assemblage

assemblage
THE ART OF THE ROOM

SHANNON McGRATH + ANNIE REID

with MARCUS PIPER

C O N T

E N T S

assemblage

The act of
bringing together a
collection of things
or people

.

WELCOME TO THE WONDERFUL WORD *ASSEMBLAGE*, AN UNUSUAL ART TERM TO DESCRIBE HOW DIFFERENT THINGS ARE ASSEMBLED.

This book applies assemblage to the world of interiors, and how elements and objects from furniture, fittings, landscape and fashion come together to transform a room into a work of art.

Great houses aren't born, they are made. They have a language and stories brought to life by the incredible talents whose work is showcased within them. Shannon McGrath has photographed many of these, within Australia's most beautiful houses over the last twenty-five years.

Each chapter begins in conversation with Annie Reid and the house's architect, designer or owner. The houses were drawn from Shannon's archive, carefully chosen for their enduring and unique qualities and then brought to life on the page by Marcus Piper.

Within those conversations, others arose about the crafted moments within each space: artwork in entries, vessels on tables, murals on walls. It became obvious that to truly explore the art of a room we needed to delve deeper. So, over many months, we slowly deconstructed each house, creating 'spin-off' stories with the artisans and makers of various objects, artworks and furniture within each house, which you'll read about.

In some projects, it was clear what each spin-off would be. In others, we were guided and delightfully led. A final flourish is the custom 'fleuron' - a little typographic symbol - created by Marcus that gives each house its own identity, adding another detail to the design.

Together, this book became a journey for the three of us in the same way we hope it is for you too. At every stage, our guiding light was assembling a new creative language, as words, images and design elevate the rich layers of each room and space as you explore each chapter and page.

Assemblage celebrates beautiful design by showing that even small things can make an extraordinary impact. We believe that now more than ever, unique objects speak to us through rich storytelling and beautiful craftsmanship.

Ultimately, we hope the book will inspire you to find your own places to create joy and magic.

ANCIENT GROUNDING

PERMANENT, PLAYFUL, SOFT

STONE SOUL HOUSE

—

ROBSON RAK ARCHITECTURE & INTERIORS

+

JOHN YOUNG | ARTIST
DANIEL BARBERA | ARTIST
TONY DEL GRECO | FORMANOVA
HELEN REDMOND | ARTIST
MEGAN DICKS AND HANNAH ABBOTT | OTOMYS

"

WE INTRODUCED INTRICATE JEWELLERY-LIKE DETAILS IN THE HOUSE.

—— *Kathryn Robson* | *architect* + *Chris Rak* | *interior architect* ——

The stories of this monolithic house extend back thousands of years,
starting with the rich limestone that lines much of its structure.

'The stone houses fossils that whisper their own stories,' Kathryn Robson says,
the co-director of Robson Rak Architecture & Interiors, alongside Chris Rak.
'You can tell the story of time just by looking at the stone – it's like a fabric or tapestry.'

Also built with handmade bricks, the home exudes permanence and solidity
across three levels and is strong enough to withstand the elements – both the weather
and the family who lives here.

But it also speaks a language that feels light, soulful and playful. Surrounded by elegant
landscaping and punctuated with courtyards and light courts, the home showcases
beautifully curved walls, stairs and brick arches that are complemented by a softening of
interior details by the artists, craftspeople and makers who have brought it to life.

'The vision was not so much about a look or style; it was more about feel and
the value in the well-made,' Rak says.

Key to the design is the datum line that runs around the house, internally and externally.
Transitioning from limestone to brick, this not only breaks up the visual bulk of
the building but also creates elements of fine detail, including the gently
curved wall upon entry.

'When you walk in the front door, you also look at treetops that are growing up from a
floor cut out down to the basement,' Rak says.

Beyond, there are zones for private use, study, work, health, fitness and entertaining,
softened by more green areas brimming with foliage, paying homage to the vernacular
of the Mediterranean home.

Artisan details add a further layer of embellishment. Almost every element has been
custom created, from the joinery to the lighting, including tables, loose furniture,
joinery pulls, art and sculpture.

Adding a layer is furniture maker, Thomas Lentini, who crafted a 'very fun' green-emerald
quartzite coffee table and round kitchen dining table. The emerald quartzite was the last
slab left in Victoria at the time and is now a piece of sculptural, crafted history.

'They all offer a delicate touch and are all just so beautiful,' Robson says.

———

Eschewing white walls for limestone, the Stone Soul House provides an unexpected platform for art,
including Maringka Baker's work, *Minyma kutjara tjukurpa*, and tables by Studio Thomas Lentini.

John Young's artwork *Aleph* hangs at the entrance. He was commissioned by Kathryn Robson and worked closely with her, using a different mindset from when he's creating work for a museum or gallery.

'It was great to see the house first and understand what was necessarily going to work sensorially and emotionally in that space for the people living there. Ultimately, it is my hope the work is affective to their daily life in the most unconscious way,' Young says.

The beauty of the work lies in its power to soften the robust architecture, through Young's highly bespoke production process. To create it, he scanned 1000 random images into a computer, including personal photos he'd taken of markets he'd visited on his travels.

'Overnight, the computer changed this into abstract forms to leave a resonance, removing the representation, but with abstract forms still resonating the colours of the markets – the memorable spices and stone colours,' he says.

He and his assistants then painted by hand that intricate, transformed image onto Belgian linen. 'There's something very special about the hand replicating these forms in oil paint, with minute gestures that reflect how the body is involved in the making,' he says.

He applies the same process to each piece, exploring what the body is saying when it is involved in the making, and using his part-digital part-handmade realisation to bring the owners' worldview into the work too.

'I call all my work of late "human technology friendship", trying to look at what's left after technology takes over from our way of working, as we evolve,' he says.

"

A VARIED EXPERIENCE UNFOLDS FROM THE FRONT DOOR AS YOU WALK INTO THE HOUSE.

—— *John Young* | *artist* ——

"

IT REALLY WAS INSPIRED BY WALKING ON THE BEACH AND LOOKING AT ROCKS. I LOVE AGE IN OBJECTS.

—— *Daniel Barbera* | *artist* ——

With his background as an industrial designer, Daniel Barbera is drawn to
function-driven design and engineering merged with heart.
But when it came to the entrance to the Stone Soul House, little did he realise that
Robson Rak's commission for a custom door pull would spark an entirely new range,
Fermat, and a creative departure from his large-object works.

'It's useful beauty,' he says. 'I love age in objects, because if you can design something that
looks better with age, it's more likely to stay in use and function.'

Cast from liquid bronze metal straight out of a mould, the handle starts as a rough
material before being machined, polished, ground and finished. Each process is completed
by hand, and each handle is different, with a mottled patina, often with sand birthmarks.
Afterwards, it is engineered with internal components to fit its door.

Once installed, the handle's surface reacts to the oils and acids of the skin,
adding an extra layer of beauty.

'You finish the handle just by touching it, and I think that's quite beautiful,' Barbera says.

As a child tinkering in his dad's workshop, Barbera was always creating things, only
realising in early high school that industrial design was a profession.

'I knew then exactly what I was going to do,' he laughs.

His collection of hardware and furniture pieces imbues a sense of softness and a lost-in-
time feeling that also reflect his love for understanding people and the environment.

'You're always seeing beauty in nature,' he says.

A beautiful moment in the Stone Soul House is the series of elegant, stadium-shaped glass and brass spinning screens, which pivot, dividing the open-plan kitchen, living and dining space from the formal sitting room.

Created by Formanova, they embody precision engineering, and they soften the house's robust stone. Each component was assessed, prototyped and tested in collaboration with the builder, glazier and joiner, with the mechanicals completely concealed while allowing for both load and functionality, along with seamlessly welded brass joins.

'We aim for effortless, everyday use. And those screens are close to perfection,' founder and CEO, Tony Del Greco says.

Growing up in southern Italy, Del Greco found metalwork to be both practical and creative. Whether he was modifying tractor components, helping to manage the family's vineyards and olive groves or finding smart ways to speed up his paper round, there was always a process that could be resolved mechanically. Most of all, he loved working with his hands to create things.

'When you grow up doing certain things in a certain way, you don't see that as out of the ordinary or exceptional,' he says.

It was after he emigrated to Australia in the 1980s that he saw an opportunity to introduce a piece of Italy – 'architectural metalwork' – to the local market. He launched Formanova in 1991.

Since his son Greg joined the business, Formanova is truly a family affair, with both committed to enhancing projects through their fastidious nature and enduring commitment to their craft.

"

IT HAS TO BE A SHOWPIECE AS WELL AS A FUNCTIONAL PIECE OF WORK.

Tony Del Greco | *Formanova*

"

IN THE SPACE OF NOTHINGNESS, THERE IS EVERYTHING.

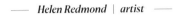

Helen Redmond | *artist*

While the limestone anchors the Stone Soul House to its site, the interior is softened and elevated to another level by a sublime selection of art.

In the family room, artist Helen Redmond's work, *Kunsthalle*, embodies her approach exploring the less obvious, quieter and calmer elements of space and time through an awareness of the Japanese architectural concepts of *ma*, the space between things, and *yohaku*, the beauty of empty space. The importance of negative space and expressing this silent language are at the core of how she communicates her work and story.

'I was drawn to the Buddhist concept of nothingness, the empty space that allows living to occur or the silent pause that communicates without words,' she says. 'My paintings try to capture the beauty and emotion of empty spaces, the nothingness that actually contains everything.'

For Redmond, 'everything' represents the transience of life and light. Using limited colours, detailed surface finishes and veils of translucent paint, she depicts liminal or transitional spaces such as corridors, light wells and architectural voids.

The works are deceptively simple. They draw you in and hold you as you try to explore what lies behind or within them. 'I want people to have to sit with the painting over time, and continually find something in it,' she says. 'To think about what is in an empty space.'

In 2012, she surprised colleagues and friends by leaving her successful career in publishing to attend art school, fulfilling a lifelong dream; she had always found solace in drawing when she needed respite.

Her unique way of observing space after thirty years as an architecture writer and interiors stylist caught the eye not only of her fellow students, who would come and sit with her in her space to enjoy 'a bit of calm in the chaos of art school', but also of her tutors, who recognised her spatial aptitude and encouraged her to delve deeper.

'The works play on perspective to create three-dimensional depth,' she says. 'You enter the painting, which is why it also works so well in architectural spaces, because it can make a room appear larger.'

Each piece comes to life in her Sydney studio, an old, corrugated-iron workshop that echoes the woolshed on the sheep station she grew up on. The surfaces of the canvases are painstakingly built up over weeks and often months, inspired by the abstract geometric qualities of modernist architecture, particularly brutalism, through which she can explore angles, shapes and lines.

In her painting, she has found a vehicle to express her creativity. 'I jumped in the deep end,' she laughs. 'I wanted to see if I could make it more than a hobby.'

———

Helen Redmond's dreamy work, *Kunsthalle*, is a delightful contrast to the spiky vases by Sally Kent above it and 'very fun' green-emerald quartzite table by Studio Thomas Lentini, below *Drum Vessel* by Clae Studio.

Redmond is represented by Megan Dicks and Hannah Abbott of Otomys, the gallerist founded in 2010 that nurtures and represents the careers of more than seventy Australian and international artists, including Greg Wood.

Although Redmond's brutalist architectural spaces and Wood's non-built form landscapes are diametrically opposed in many respects, the language behind them is similar.

'Both Redmond and Wood employ colour and light to evoke a sense of intrigue and wonderment,' Dicks says.

She believes there is an intrinsic link between artists and residential interiors. In the same way that our homes are laden with personal narratives, vessels for memories and objects collected over time, so too are artworks.

'Incorporating art that speaks to our emotions and understanding of the world is a vital part of building a home that reflects the values of the inhabitants. Art connects us to memory, not simply ours, but the artist's, and the world captured at that moment in time,' Abbott says.

In the Stone Soul House, each piece of work is both anchored and elevated by the strong permanence of Robson Rak's architecture. If only those limestone walls could talk.

"

A HOME IS JUST LIKE AN ARTWORK.

—— *Megan Dicks and Hannah Abbott* | *Otomys* ——

———

V6 Nature of Change by Greg Wood echoes the tones and earthy palette in a quiet moment in the Stone Soul House.

LIGHT TOUCH

UTILITY, ELEGANCE, CRAFT

COLLECTORS DEN

—

HECKER GUTHRIE

+

GUY PHELAN | CABINET-MAKER

"

I LOVE THE NOSTALGIA, THE CHARM, THE LOST CRAFT.

Paul Hecker | *interior designer*

Paul Hecker, interior designer and co-director of Hecker Guthrie, bought his home in 2011, when it was 103 years old, never intending to live there. But times and circumstances change. Initially, he desired to simply renovate a period house to sell, but over time it became evident he was renovating it to live in.

'The house and its five handsomely proportioned rooms drew me in,' he says. 'The intricate arts and crafts fireplaces and ornate plaster ceilings all played a part in the seduction – a place to create a world of my own.'

Inside, Hecker embraces the idea of a series of cosy rooms, each with a distinct personality. He aimed to 'tread lightly', with his intervention in the original house being as gentle as possible; no walls were relocated or period details removed.

In the kitchen, modern minimalist appliances sit in stark contrast to a more sympathetic approach to 'joinery as furniture', which can be removed and repurposed, leaving the original room intact.

The palette is a series of greens, ranging from a sombre, dark khaki in the front living room to a more playful Robin Hood green in the pantry.

Unlike most, Hecker doesn't fully embrace light and bright, finding himself drawn to darker, more cosy, intimate spaces.

'If I want sunlight, I can go outside,' he quips.

The house has become a vehicle for him to display his ever-growing collection of 'stuff'. Vignettes and carefully curated displays of objects and artefacts decorate each room, the product of hours of browsing through auction rooms. Intellectually, he's a minimalist; emotionally, he's the opposite.

Dutch Delftware sits with English arts and crafts Royal Doulton, and 1970s Australian pottery exists happily next to 1950s and 60s Danish Royal Copenhagen ceramics. The house is filled with objects that can't be recreated; for example, Schneider and Gallé art glass lamps nestle on tables with Rosenberg porcelain from the Netherlands.

———

Paul Hecker in his arts and crafts home, built in 1908, beside the Greg Wood work, *Mowbrays/Dryden*.

'For me, the joy comes from finding the beauty in an object that others can't see.
Often, that speaks to a lost craft or lost techniques of manufacture.
I love giving found objects new life,' he says.

While he admits his love of general knowledge takes him down the odd rabbit hole
on occasions – he once bought six Victorian bird feeders at an auction,
intrigued by the notion of becoming an instant expert – the thrill of the chase
and the opportunity to learn take over.

'I tend to start collecting something, try and become knowledgeable, purchase madly and
then at an unspecified point, realise I have enough, and then relax. Until next time.'

His love for craft extended to the joinery fittings and furniture within the home.
He worked closely with his builder, Sam Persson, and cabinet-maker, Guy Phelan,
to ensure that all works spoke to the tradition of the home. Phelan crafted joinery
for the kitchen, pantry, bedroom and bathroom that resembles bespoke pieces
of furniture, designed to patina over time.

Like the objects, the furniture is an eclectic collection, and while it is not to everyone's
taste, Hecker has created a home that quietly fills him with joy every day.

'I feel that anyone could walk into my home and, without knowing me, would know who
I am ... This home is me!' he laughs.

"

FOR ME, THE JOY COMES FROM FINDING THE BEAUTY IN AN OBJECT THAT OTHERS CAN'T SEE.

Layers of objects from an era or artist are grouped in Paul Hecker's home,
from his Acqua Di Parma products on the mantelpiece (opposite, bottom right) to his collection of
Dutch Gouda Ware ceramics bought at various auctions (opposite, bottom left).

All the joinery for Hecker's house was built by cabinet-maker Guy Phelan using traditional methods of construction. The bathroom cabinet, kitchen cabinets, pantry, bedroom chest of drawers, hallway cupboard and laundry were all constructed as if they were furniture pieces; solid timber features heavily, and all hinges and hardware are traditional brass components. The furniture is built to last and patina, completely at home in an arts and crafts house from 1908.

Hecker's house was their first collaboration, and while Phelan now works with other designers on select residential projects, it was this one that helped springboard his career.

'Everyone was on the same page and the build was fun,' he says.

Phelan likes the challenge of working with solid timber, crafting joinery and furniture pieces that last.

'It's still a tree. It's not alive, but depending on the seasons it expands and retracts and there's a bit more skill with solid timber,' he says.

A third-generation carpenter, Phelan worked with both his grandfather and his father as a young cabinet-maker and joiner but was almost destined to become a chef before he turned to woodworking.

He is now well known for exactly that, and his approach with Hecker made for a perfect partnership. They didn't need complicated drawings to understand the brief, and they shared an understanding of craft in which simple materials, traditional making and handpainting formed the process for creating objects designed as pieces of furniture.

'He allowed the project to unfold, and he put full trust in my craft,' Phelan says.

In doing so, they have created a home with interiors that embrace light and dark with effortless ease, yet can easily be dismantled depending on its next life.

"

YOU CAN'T COMPARE FLATPACK TO A BEAUTIFUL PIECE OF FURNITURE THAT IS SOLID TIMBER.

—— *Guy Phelan* | *cabinet-maker* ——

LIVING TREASURES

ARTFUL, ATMOSPHERIC, VIBRANT

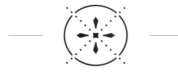

VILLA GLEN

—

LUCY CLEMENGER ARCHITECTS

+

GEORGIE BRUCE | HOUSE OWNER
NATALIE JAMES | STYLIST
CHRIS HADDAD | ARCHIER

Lucy Clemenger selected several of Le Corbusier's colours, including 32034 from his 1931 collection, used in the sitting room (top left and bottom right), crafting a platform for objects, including a Moooi Meshmatics chandelier (top right) and pebble oval pendant by Mark Douglass Design, which Georgie Bruce chose for the main bedroom (bottom left).

"

THE ELEMENTS OF THE PAST THAT HAVE A STORY MAKE ALL THE CONTEMPORARY PIECES WORK SO WELL.

—— *Lucy Clemenger* | *architect* ——

Lucy Clemenger is well known for her philosophy of refined sensibility. As the director of Lucy Clemenger Architects, her challenge for Villa Glen was to stitch many eclectic moments into a cohesive response that felt considered, yet highly distinctive.

'It's a really beautiful home full of the family's living treasures, collected from their travels and journeys,' she says.

The house owner, Georgie Bruce, engaged Clemenger to rethink the home's clunky footprint and poor internal functionality and to create better sightlines by which to view her substantial collection of contemporary artworks, sculptures and objects collected in a lifelong dedication to art.

To create a new language for the house, Clemenger wound the clock back to 1931, connecting two significant moments in time.

Firstly, in that year, architect and painting luminary Le Corbusier had just published his great work *Le Corbusier: Polychromie architecturale*, a unique tool for colour selection made specifically for architecture interiors and presenting his ideas on how harmonious tones could embody spatial effects and arouse reactions. As a result, Le Corbusier designed two new colour palettes, in 1931 and 1959 respectively, comprising sixty-three shades overall. His theory centred on three key ideas: using synthetic pigments for contrast, employing natural colours for atmosphere and implementing transparent synthetic pigments to change surfaces without impacting how the eye sees spatial depth. They were systematic, with colours full of life, hugely intense and yet reservedly elegant.

Secondly, Villa Glen was built in 1931.

Clemenger's design narrative was born.

Her first step was selecting from Le Corbusier's 1931 palette, which, most interestingly, was designed to be combined in any manner. Together, she and Bruce chose core colours of green, blue and a pink base and then positioned the colours in rooms throughout the house, choosing pink tiles in the bathroom close to colour 32111 and blue bathroom tiles as close to colour 32030. Clemenger then photographed all of Bruce's artworks and placed them in drawings to scale, to show their suitability alongside the selected colours. In this way, the colours, as a backdrop, were made to be as important as the art. They were complemented by subtle art deco accents in brass and marble.

'I know Georgie likes to move things around all the time too, so when you go there, it's totally changed, and you read the energy of the space differently,' Clemenger says.

The result is a bold collection of artworks and spaces that differ wildly yet together appear seamless within Clemenger's highly considered colour palette. It's big, colourful and full of life – exactly as intended.

As a visual art consultant, art manager and curator of her business, GB Art Advisory, Georgie Bruce brings the same energy to her clients and business life – and into her Villa Glen home. For Bruce, art is energy. It gives life, stimulates conversation and engagement and tells different stories on multiple levels.

'My style isn't monochrome. We didn't want a typical one-colour palette as a family,' she says.

When planning her renovation with Lucy Clemenger Architects, she loved the idea of employing colour theory not only to evoke emotion based on science but also to help create better visual lines to experience her art.

Bruce spent months advising, hanging and placing each art piece, orienting furniture to optimise each room's circulation and focusing on the finer details such as specific door types and heights. Her insight helped to inform how each piece might work with the colour palette, creating a richness to the reading of each space.

'We approached the layout as if we were working on the temporary walls of a gallery and how you might view corridors and read the artwork,' she says. 'How do we create curated views across and between spaces?'

Artworks from Korea, Japan and China are peppered amongst works by Indigenous Australian and contemporary artists, layered in harmonious groupings to create cross-cultural exchange, impact and engagement. Despite the pieces' varying ages, mediums, artists and countries of origin, they present effortlessly through Clemenger's Le Corbusier–inspired colour palette.

The home reflects Bruce's life story: she lived in northern Asia for eleven years and has twenty-five years of experience in both Asian and Australian art.

'We can now appreciate our beautiful collection and experience everything in one space, at the one time,' she says.

"

WE APPROACHED THE LAYOUT AS IF WE WERE WORKING ON THE TEMPORARY WALLS OF A GALLERY AND HOW YOU MIGHT VIEW CORRIDORS AND READ THE ARTWORK.

Georgie Bruce | *house owner*

TSANG Kin-Wah's work, *Fucking Art Made by the Fucking People and for the Fucking People*, comprises botanical word art, creating lively conversations over the dining table as the words are deciphered.

"

I'M DRAWN TO THE PEOPLE AND THEIR THINGS WHEN I WORK, BEFORE THE ARCHITECTURE AND THE LINES.

—— *Natalie James* | *stylist* ——

When Shannon McGrath recommended stylist Natalie James to collaborate with Clemenger on Bruce's home, it was a perfect match.

'I do love to bring colour to a project,' James laughs.

James brings to her stylist work her major influences, being art – naming Henri Matisse for his bold colour, the places she has travelled to and her Polish heritage. She also draws on her passion for travel and a nostalgic sense of warmth and cosiness from her childhood home.

'Villa Glen was about finishing the rooms' sentences. Giving them a little more layering and creating more depth using the art as inspiration,' she says.

Specifically, James focused on the dining room, introducing six differently coloured Osso dining chairs by Ronan & Erwan Bouroullec.

'When selecting, there was only one of each colour, but I felt that was exactly what the room needed, to play on Georgie's sense of fun, and adding a great conversation piece. A "happy accident",' she says.

In the lounge, she installed her personal and previously owned green velvet sofa, an original 1970s Fler modular, which she spotted on a hard-rubbish pile and had reupholstered. Other objects and ceramics were included to complement Bruce's artworks and colour palette.

When James steps inside someone else's home, her greatest joy is finding inspiration from the things they've collected to make a space feel more 'meaningful'.

'Often, people will say they don't know what their style is. I say that your style is all the things that you love, and if you collect all the things that you love and put them together, they'll probably work for you,' she says.

For Clemenger, Archier's Capital pendant was the perfect choice to suspend above the 8-metre-long marble kitchen bench, to engage with as a sculptural object whether it was switched on or off.

It features a fluted brass profile and American walnut timber detailing and gives a subtle nod to art deco and New York design. Upon closer inspection, its design mirrors the building blocks of a building plan, as Archier co-director, Chris Haddad explains.

'It has a central extrusion of aluminium and LED lighting strip, which, using a building as an analogy, is akin to the service core, and then the outside extruded brass profile is like the cladding. The idea was to be able to interchange different cladding onto the central core, which would allow variations and bespoke pieces to be created easily.'

While busy with architecture and design work, Archier has never strayed from the immediate, hands-on nature of workshop production: prototyping, experimenting and making. The practice has two pendants in production: the Highline, a recessive light designed to let the architecture speak, and the Capital, its statement showpiece.

'The pendant has a distinct architectural quality that complements the building it is within, of quality and timelessness,' Haddad says.

The young, dynamic architecture and design studio is also led by Chris Gilbert, Josh FitzGerald and landscape architect Jon Kaitler. In addition to running a more traditional architecture studio, they have always had access to workshops and sculpture studio spaces where they can continue their focus on designing raw, subtle interior objects that contribute to a better quality of life.

For now, the practice is exploring design and technology with its timber prefabrication business and automation using robotics.

'While the industry is a slow adopter of new technologies, it's an exciting space,' Haddad says.

At Villa Glen, Clemenger, Bruce, James and Haddad have combined their design skill to craft a home that inspires conversations and lifts the art of living in colour to new heights.

"

YOU ENGAGE WITH IT AS AN OBJECT.

—— *Chris Haddad* | *Archier* ——

Archier's Capital pendant is suspended elegantly over the island bench, under which sit timber Tractor stools.

ETHEREAL HEIGHTS

SWEEPING, CURVILINEAR, ABSTRACT

AVIAN APARTMENT

—

ALICIA HOLGAR INTERIORS

+

STEVEN JOHN CLARK AND LARS STOTEN | DENHOLM

"

EVERY LITTLE PIECE IS IMPORTANT AND TELLS A STORY.

—— *Alicia Holgar* | *designer* ——

When the interior you're engaged to refresh is within an iconic waterfront property by Australian architect Harry Seidler, how do you build upon existing beauty?

Director, Alicia Holgar began with Seidler himself, whose design fingerprints are all over the building, with his signature sweeping curves, minimal ornamentation and characterful gestures.

'I dug pretty deep,' she laughs. She immersed herself in Seidler's world and leaned into his design philosophy of modernist substance through the amalgamation of aesthetics, function and technology. In this building, he integrated all three with an articulate play on curves and cantilevers.

With heritage protections restricting any external work, Holgar was also briefed to leave the kitchen, bathrooms and marble flooring untouched. That left the interior layers which she renewed with pure lines, elegant forms and custom-made pieces designed by Holgar herself, alongside other makers in the sweeping sofa, granite coffee table, solid American oak timber bookshelves, custom joinery and study desk, enriching the substance without bringing the bling.

The showstopper is the 5-metre-long, cantilevered, sweeping wall that slices through the centre of the floor plan. On one side it carves out space for a dining room and on the other creates a corridor that reveals the apartment's bedrooms.

While this freed up a wall for furnishing, Holgar felt that hanging a piece of substantial art there didn't feel quite right.

'I leafed through the archives and found that Seidler had experimented with wall murals in his work. I thought this would be an interesting way to integrate art with architecture,' she says.

That led her to Jessalyn Brooks, a Los Angeles–based artist and painter who often depicts the contours of the female form in works that are subtle and loose, blocky and abstract.

Brooks flew to Australia for the commission but didn't commit to the design until she could physically inhabit the space, according to Holgar.

'She was looking out over the skyline, and it felt like being up in the sky in the clouds, with the birds,' Holgar says. Brooks created the wall mural called *The Avians*, featuring bird-like or flying creatures that in Greek mythology represent power, freedom and wisdom.

'It evolved into this really beautiful interpretation of people living up in the sky,' Holgar says. 'This piece tells a story, and it feels quite ethereal.'

———

Alicia Holgar beside her custom-designed lounge and a large work, *RH 245 Downtown* by Ryan Hoffmann.

Frank Gehry's classic Wiggle Side Chair, for Vitra, sits nearby a white sculpture by Walter Auer, accentuating the curvilinear language.

Near the entry, a tactile, pebble-twisted table greets visitors to the Avian Apartment. It was one of DenHolm's very first designs.

With little other than a mood board, images of Jessalyn Brooks's mural and loose proportions in their heads, the co-directors and artists, Steven John Clark and Lars Stoten, began as they usually do, drawing a line on their studio wall.

'It's the beginning and the reference to the direction of the piece,' Stoten says. 'The drawing informs the process, and then it becomes quite organic.'

DenHolm uses Australian limestone cut straight off the seabed and produces each item of furniture entirely by hand, chipping, carving and playing with a host of pieces – usually about sixteen at the start – before beginning to apply, stack and edit them.

They draw another shape, this time a clock face, on the floor around the piece. This enables them to walk around it, constantly assessing, to see how close it is to its final format and the inbuilt structure they'll use to hold it together.

'I never really want the client to know exactly what it looks like on the other side. That way, it keeps you always engaged,' Clark says, recalling that this particular table would speak to the curving Harry Seidler walls of the apartment it was to live in.

Clark and Stoten are currently focused on widening their practice, experimenting with materials like polyfoam, glass and bronze, as well as with techniques such as silvering and rubber-dipping.

'I can safely say no one does what we do in the world with limestone, but for the first time we've got freedom also outside of it, so we're pretty excited to play,' Stoten says.

It's also a design response that Harry Seidler may have felt perfectly at ease with.

"

I WANT IT TO REVEAL ITSELF DIFFERENTLY AS YOU WALK AROUND IT.

—— *Steven John Clark and Lars Stoten* | *DenHolm* ——

WHIMSICAL FEELS

MOODY, SOFT, ALLURING

PARKLIFE APARTMENT

—

HECKER GUTHRIE

+

DEL KATHRYN BARTON | ARTIST
HENRY WILSON | STUDIO HENRY WILSON

"

I THINK THIS IS WHERE THE JOY LIES. CELEBRATING PLACE, WHILE CREATING A HEIGHTENED EXPERIENCE THROUGH A VERY PERSONAL DESIGN RESPONSE.

—— *Hamish Guthrie* | *interior designer* ——

Apartments in tall buildings have different design rules. Without grand heights or big footprints to fall back on, often it's about the views. But when a couple engaged Hecker Guthrie's interior designer and co-director, Hamish Guthrie to downsize to a three-bedroom city apartment from a large Victorian home, he had to think carefully.

'It can't be just about the view,' he says. 'How do we create a bespoke interior response which connects at both a physical and sensory level, creating a series of unique spaces that resonate with the owners' whims and passions?'

With their background in medical science, the owners are also avid art collectors and were keen to create a canvas upon which to showcase new and old pieces. Guthrie used this as the starting point, creating a dark, moody interior distinct from the white aesthetic of their former Victorian terrace and the breezy vibes of their coastal home.

'They felt it was an opportunity to have a new lease on life,' he says.

The apartment went under the knife, enabling Guthrie to layer his fine crafts approach. Some of the pokier sections were opened up, while the surfaces were reduced to just three materials: stone, timber and textured render. The harder apartment edges were also ironed out to create a seamless connection, with a softer, sculptural feel between floor and ceiling. Loose furniture was used to delineate spaces without requiring walls to move, while timber joinery in the kitchen and bathrooms was introduced to bring warmth.

Importantly, the flattened palette lets the artworks punch through the spaces. Most pieces were preselected during the briefing stage, and fresh works were brought in for the renovated apartment to blend old and new.

The standout piece, *Oh intervene for us* by Del Kathryn Barton, occupies almost the full height of the wall in the main living room. Others are more subtle, including Studio Henry Wilson's Surface Wall Sconce. And while the aspects across lush, green parkland beyond are still part of the apartment experience, the artwork takes precedence.

'I think this is where the joy lies,' Guthrie says. 'Celebrating place, while creating a heightened experience through a very personal design response.'

Archibald Prize–winning artist Del Kathryn Barton has long featured and celebrated
narratives around the female form, often whimsical, sumptuous and surreal,
and sometimes psychedelic.

While her mixed-media, large-scale work *Oh intervene for us* in the living room was created
in 2006, its core themes of longing and the dichotomy of vulnerability with strength are
just as compelling in her practice today.

'Ultimately, the female form's desire for connection is an inexplicable and universal sort
of human experience,' she says.

The piece is particularly special because it speaks to her personal life at the time,
as a mother working from home with two very young children. And it's rare, because
she hasn't often produced large works on paper in recent years, although paper remains
a central part of her drawing practice.

'I always feel a much greater level of freedom. There's a glorious element of play, constant
interrogation and growth of my aesthetic sensibilities,' she says.

She currently works from a separate commercial studio as a multidisciplinary artist – and
filmmaker – using pigment liners, ink, glass and watercolour, along with fabric, in particular
Italian dupion silk, which she used to border the work displayed in the living room.

Each piece is made in a controlled, private place before it enters the world on its own
terms, independent of other creative disciplines.

'I see it as a great privilege and a great honour that the work makes it into the world and
especially into really loving homes,' she says.

"

IT'S THAT AUTHENTIC, RAW, HONEST HUMAN ENGAGEMENT AND EXCHANGE.

— *Del Kathryn Barton* | *artist* —

———

Del Kathryn Barton's *Oh intervene for us* embodies not just an entire wall but also Hecker Guthrie's
response to add layers beyond the apartment's sweeping views.

Hecker Guthrie's dark, moody palette is accented by gentle pops of light and colour, including one of two Julia Ciccarone works, *Mesmerised* (opposite), and soft lighting in the drinks alcove (above).

"

THERE'S A BRUTAL OBVIOUSNESS AND HONESTY IN THE FORM AND MATERIAL CHOICE.

Henry Wilson | *Studio Henry Wilson*

Finally in the kitchen, Studio Henry Wilson's Surface Wall Sconce appears unobtrusively affixed to a wall. Of all the lighting, furniture, objects and hardware pieces in his portfolio, these have proved the most popular. He launched the collection in 2018 and the light has evolved into both wall and shelf applications, comprising combinations of stone and metal, each with a unique finish designed to patina over time.

'I feel there's a certain honesty imbued in my design, which I think is pleasing for people because they can respond to it. It has a naivety to the form and construction,' Wilson says.

He's taken a somewhat different path from his early education in industrial design, in which he trained in all manner of items, ranging from toothbrushes to airline seats. Ultimately, that left him feeling unfulfilled.

'I found a simpatico with other kinds of objects. It scratches a more creative itch in me that is probably more expressive and better defined as an industrial arts practice,' he says.

His pieces are highly sculptural, ambient and robust. He works with metals, including brass, bronze and stainless steel, as well as timbers, stone, leather and glass in his studio, where the process of casting and production is lengthy.

While he's fascinated by the imperfections in his work during the production process, he also enjoys exploring tension as materials are added together.

'It's playing in the subconscious,' he says. 'And it's about trying to design things that shift how people think about the objects they live with.'

For the couple who now call this apartment home, their whims are fulfilled and their walls are enriched by artists who bring to life the art of tension and play.

———

Made from black travertine, Studio Henry Wilson's Surface Wall Sconce adds a layer of textured beauty in the kitchen.

GRAND UNVEILING

BALANCED, EMOTIVE, CAPTIVATING

THE GLASS HOUSE

—

ADDARC

+

SARAH FLETCHER | FLETCHER ARTS
RICHARD STRINGER | ARTIST
JACK MERLO | HOUSE OWNER

"

THE HOUSE IS SUCH A BEAUTIFUL SPACE AND A LABOUR OF LOVE FOR MANY YEARS.

—— *Tamara Dunkley and Rohan Appel* | *architects* ——

A long, monolithic box sits elegantly above the street at the end of a leafy cul-de-sac.
Its facade shimmers with thousands of hand-cut, hand-installed, clear glass bricks – 4923,
to be exact. By day, the glass-brick screen ushers the sun inside beautifully.
By night, it creates a veil of translucence that softly silhouettes the inhabitants
while accentuating a canopy of greenery in front.

It is an epic home that speaks a language of sculpture and scale, and its joy is found in the
interplay between hard and soft, light and landscape, meticulously crafted by ADDARC's
co-directors Tamara Dunkley and Rohan Appel, owned by their client, landscape designer,
Jack Merlo. The brief was to design a large home for Merlo and his family, whose love of
art and landscape is reflected on a grand scale.

The home comprises two long, L-shaped blocks at the front, one atop the other, leaving
enough land behind for a pool, barbeque area and generous landscaping.

The interior is focused on a central spine and a dramatic double-height gallery atrium
space, which extends from the front entry door through to the rear. Given the vertical
height of the space, Dunkley and Appel knew they needed something spectacular to
celebrate the spine and began to play with Vibia lighting modules.
Each light works on a solid rod suspension, and they selected a configuration of
four individual fittings, each with drop pendants.

'It almost creates this constellation where each one becomes its own pin starlight,'
Appel says.

From the spine, generous spaces flow across each level; from formal living and dining
to relaxed entertaining and kitchen, including a basement with a wine-tasting room
and guest suite. Upstairs, a glazed bridge links to the children's wing, with bedrooms,
ensuites and rumpus. Each space is distinctly separate but beautifully resolved,
with access to natural light at every opportunity.

'The ground-floor plane is quite dark, so having this ephemeral, light-filled top, particularly
with the glass bricks, makes it much more spacious,' Appel says.

———

Below the Vibia lighting modules and handcut glass bricks, the Glass House entry reveals Guan Wei's
bronze sculpture, *Cloud No. 3* alongside Bruce Armstrong's *Bunjil.*

Nearby in the dining room, a taxidermy peacock appears on a bed of flowers atop a twenty-two seat dining table, the result of an irresistible opportunity for Dunkley.

With her interest in floristry as well as architecture, she found the peacock in a neighbourhood florist's shop and brought it to the Glass House to introduce a sense of scale commensurate with the opulence of the banquet-style dining setting.

'Wouldn't it be amazing if we could style something around these incredible tail feathers?' she suggested.

With quinces and cactuses and many concealed zip ties, the peacock appears at home in its position, and Dunkley got to indulge her creative freedom in a riff on tradition.

'My mum was very much into flowers and floral arranging growing up, and I was too. I had a part-time job working in a twenty-four-hour florist, so I'd come home from working in the office and then work in the florist overnight,' she says.

She's attracted to the powerful impact that a space can hold and the ability to create a talking point through a composition that draws the eye in, using her work in architecture or her passion for floristry. Whether through a plant or a colour or even something as simple as a glass vase full of cactuses, her floral work enables her to express a different side of her creativity, bringing a sense of sculptural colour, style and impermanence.

"

LET'S MAKE IT SOMETHING CRAZY.

—— *Tamara Dunkley* | *architect* ——

Richard Stringer's *The Queen is Dead* sits next to the Taccia table lamp by Achille and Pier Giacomo
Castiglioni for FLOS (opposite).
The Glass House features eclectic moments including Paul Wood's work, *Tiger* (top left), and brass
accents from Richard Stringer in *Untitled Maquette* (bottom right, centre).

"

IT'S CONSIDERED STORYTELLING, AND IT'S RESPECTING THE ART.

—— *Sarah Fletcher* | *Fletcher Arts* ——

ADDARC collaborated with art consultant and director of Fletcher Arts, Sarah Fletcher, to select around forty pieces for the Glass House, meticulously matching art that celebrates the architects, their styles and the house's context but equally providing an opportunity for the artists' works to shine.

Fletcher has an exquisite eye for the unusual and imperfect, and dedicates her work to securing and curating art for spaces that are effortlessly stylish but also tell a story, elevating them to another level.

'Art is just magic like that,' she says. 'It adds layers of personality.'

She has represented artist Richard Stringer for many years (as well as David Ray, Peter D Cole and Louis Grant), selling his bee replicas through her home gallery. She has a philosophy of enabling people to live with art rather than simply viewing it in a white gallery.

'Some clients are just not going to get that there's a dead bee on a building, but other collectors really care for the storytelling and know the art and the intellectual backstory behind it,' Fletcher says.

Art flows through her veins, growing up as she did with artists and creative thinkers in her house.

'My father was fascinated by people who build and create things. He was obsessed with people who could create something of value out of nothing,' she says.

Alongside his mining and farming career, her father established a syndicate backing three or four promising artists, enabling them to create without needing to support themselves financially. As a result, they doubled their expected output and became highly successful.

In turn, Fletcher pursued her creative career as a showroom director, gallery owner and an importer and distributor of furniture from France and Italy.

'I focus more on the artist now. A good artist needs to shred a lot of flesh to become good for a piece of art, and that's something incredible to give a home to,' she says.

———

Sarah Fletcher pictured in her private showroom with Richard Stringer's composite bees on the wall next to Daniel Barbera's Lovelock Coat Stand.

"

I'M INTERESTED IN HOW CITIES ARE FASHIONED BY THE SAME KIND OF MATERIALS AS NATURE.

—— *Richard Stringer* | *artist* ——

Artwork by one of Fletcher's artists, Richard Stringer, features twice in the Glass House: a bronze mountain on a plinth in the study and a small, white, cultured marble bee upside down on a building in the formal dining room, near the taxidermy peacock.

They reveal a richness in his approach to his art, in which he is fascinated politically and philosophically by how people organise themselves.

'I'm interested in how cities are fashioned by the same kind of materials as nature, whether it's stone or something else, and like any kind of colony, you build it up from the resources around you,' he says.

Across his work, the bees have proved particularly popular. The most recognised are large gold bees fixed to residential and commercial buildings, adding a high-vibe aesthetic reflecting the busy street activity below. The largest, titled *Queen Bee*, has breasts that represent the interface between architecture and society.

After the first gold bees were installed, the appetite for them grew. 'I then had a playful idea to make those little souvenirs you get in Europe, but of the bees,' he says. From a factory in Greece that produces similar products of the statue of David, he began making and selling small white replicas of his bees. He has sold thousands: 'In some ways, the bees took over my life,' he laughs.

In his studio, he's applying the finishing touches to another *Queen Bee*, entitled *Dead Bee*; this one bigger, in bronze, is now in its final resting place at a winery sculpture park in an enclosure designed by architect Nonda Katsalidis. He's also been working on other large, complicated figurative works in composite materials, which are laborious and technically challenging.

'I do my own thing, and a designer or curator may then find an appropriate position relative to the space itself,' he says.

——

Richard Stringer's aluminium bronze work *Table Mountain* is a striking piece in the dining room.

Finally, with its robust, dark interior and full-height glass throughout, Merlo's home provided the perfect opportunity for him to complement the architecture with a similarly bold approach to the landscape.

'The garden and landscapes are a backdrop to most of the internal spaces, so we were keen to have a consistency that flowed in the use of similar materials,' Merlo says, as the director of Jack Merlo Landscape Design.

He selected a light-grey limestone and charcoal granite for the hard landscaping, which flows into the infinity-edge pool. The plantings range from tailored and structural to lighter and informal.

At the front, bamboo in planters create a soft backdrop against the glass bricks, alongside three Japanese ginkgo trees – Merlo's favourite – with delicate green leaves that turn yellow in autumn.

As well as creating a private, tranquil feel, the landscape integrates seamlessly with the architecture. For example, a large, cylindrical concrete planter attached to the front path functions as a retaining wall and balustrade, but the Japanese maple and cascading greenery soften the effect.

'The sense of openness is what is really beautiful in this home. It was all designed in such a way to create an oasis,' Merlo says.

Through careful curatorship and a vision to create something out of the ordinary, the Glass House delivers both with style and dazzling brilliance.

"

THIS HOUSE WAS QUITE ADVENTUROUS.

—— *Jack Merlo* | *house owner* ——

HERITAGE SECRETS

DISCOVERY, CELEBRATION, HISTORY

COBDEN TERRACE

—

MATT GIBSON ARCHITECTURE + DESIGN

+

YVONNE CHOONG | HOUSE OWNER
ANTON ASSAAD | GREAT DANE FURNITURE

"

WE TRY TO AMPLIFY SOME OF THAT HISTORY AND THE STORYTELLING OF WHAT IS OLD AND WHAT IS NEW.

—— *Matt Gibson* | *architect* ——

When does a heritage house wholeheartedly and respectfully embody its past, present and future?

This was the challenge for director, Matt Gibson, who navigated not only the onerous state heritage protections applied to the exterior of this double-brick, double-storey, 1869-built Victorian house but also the major restrictions placed on interior works due to its national significance.

The brief was to gently equip the house with modern sensibilities for the couple who had bought it, along with their collection of mid-century art and design objects, furniture pieces and travelling memories, spanning a collective 100-year history.

Known for his beautiful conversions from old to new, Gibson's response was to rethink heritage design altogether.

'There's a sense of touching things softly and maintaining the heritage edict of reversibility,' he says.

Outside, the only addition was a small, black, zinc-clad box at the rear, containing a bathroom and laundry amenities space. It is almost disconnected from the rear brickwork at the end of the building by a small shadow gap and is designed so that it can be removed in time with very little damage to the original heritage fabric.

Within the building, the minimal changes unlocked significant functionality and included enlarging the opening to the dining room and, the most hotly debated element, removing a damaged chimney in the kitchen. This enabled better versatility within the kitchen to incorporate an island bench and create greater circulation to the rest of the house.

'It's this concept of "living heritage" and how heritage elements can be allowed to live and exist though minor tweaks while retaining their significance and memory of what they were,' Gibson says.

The physical footprint of the chimney's original brickwork on the floor has been revealed, and the entire process was documented, meaning the memory and trace of the chimney are honoured. A sense of living architecture has been created for the home's inhabitants and visitors.

Colour is also integral to the interior treatment. Mixed with brass, metal and shiny surfaces, a dark, vivid blue imbues the front living and dining rooms. In contrast, the circulation areas and kitchen are bathed in striking mustard, gold and brown tones, complemented by brass accents in almost every room.

'We surrounded one of the door portals in brass, to provide a continuity in coordinated materials and finishes throughout the house while combining that with highly individualised spaces, fittings and furniture,' Gibson says.

The final layer, the end chapter in this house's rich story, is the vintage collection of furniture, furnishings, art and objects owned by Luke Merrick and his partner, Yvonne Choong.

"

THE FURNITURE IS OF THE HOUSE – IT FEELS OLD AND LIVED IN AND COMFORTABLE AND FEMININE.

—— *Yvonne Choong* | *house owner* ——

Over several years, Yvonne Choong and Luke Merrick have slowly accumulated and created the vintage mid-century layers of their house. Choong is drawn to longevity and loves the idea of furniture and fittings that offer a sense of stability.

'I think things should be made to last,' she says. 'We just try to do things slowly and deliberately, and not rush things.'

The result is a house that beautifully balances mid-century design with heritage architecture, culminating in what Choong describes as imbuing a restful quality.

'It isn't bright, but it isn't dark either. I find it relaxing, very much like a sanctuary,' she says.

While many pieces make large-scale statements, such as the restored Poul Cadovius wall bookcase system and Le Corbusier's Lampe de Marseille, others are less obvious, but they make a big difference to how the inhabitants live. For example, there is a small, 1-metre-wide opening between the kitchen and dining room, an original moment in the house.

'This little middle passageway opening just links everything together, and we use the space in the house differently as a result,' Choong says.

———

Yvonne Choong sits beside the brickwork that honours the original chimney in the heritage home. Bold brass thresholds embellish the mustard colour tones throughout Cobden Terrace, accented by Nic Plowman's crisp artwork, *Avalanche #3* and Miyazaki Bar Stools by Inoda + Sveje.

The colour palette shifts from light to dark complemented by pieces including Greg Wood's *V2 Reimagining* on the bedroom wall (opposite) and the moodier work by Danny Cohen, *Hyena* (bottom left).

On the first floor, the house introduces layers from Great Dane Furniture, a driving force in the popularity of Scandinavian design. The classic Ring Chair by Nanna Ditzel is finished in McNutt fabric in Walnut and sits in front of the Senator Floor Lamp, by Lisa Johansson-Pape, both from Great Dane Furniture.

According to director, Anton Assaad, one – or two – pieces of furniture can make a huge difference in someone's life.

'That to me is really special,' he says. 'When you are truly bringing something special to clients that you can't find anywhere else in the world.'

Along with creative director Megan Marshall, he has dedicated his life to celebrating exactly that, discovering people around the world making unique and extraordinary products and sharing them with customers through Great Dane Furniture. Every item of furniture contains a story. It's within these stories of heritage, quality and integrity that the magic lies.

Assaad launched the business with a single vision, travelling to Denmark every ninety days to buy one-off vintage pieces – mid-century only – and shipping back two containers bursting with original furniture to sell.

But without a consistent supply, it was difficult to maintain stock levels, prompting a brave decision. He moved from vintage reselling into selling new furniture, with a vision of working with makers and factories on new products as well as putting back into production designs from retired mid-century furniture makers.

'We were very adamant that the integrity and the quality of the brand had to be preserved as a vintage sort of business,' he says.

He loves to visit factories personally – the less known the better – to see how they make things and reassure them of his commitment to their work.

'It was a lot of relationship building over a long time, but it allowed us to grow our business in a way that no one's ever been able to do,' he says.

Assaad explains it as a feeling of being comfortable enough in and around the furniture to imagine the joy of bringing home a piece that someone will truly enjoy living with in their own home.

'Someone once said to me ours is a very intimate business. You're actually in someone's house, so to speak,' he says.

With Gibson's sensitive renovation, Great Dane's furniture and the couple's love for solid design and robust elements, Cobden Terrace will create a new chapter and legacy.

"

WE'RE NOT FASHION, AND WE NEVER WILL BE.

— *Anton Assaad* | *Great Dane Furniture* —

HOTEL HOMAGE

PATTERNED, SCULPTED, ENRICHING

BALMERINO RESIDENCE

—

STUDIO GRIFFITHS ARCHITECTURE + DESIGN

+

VOLKER HAUG | VOLKER HAUG STUDIO
IRINA RYBAKOV | PÉPITE

"

IT HAS THIS LUSH LONDON VIBE.

—— *Gillianne Griffiths* | *interior architect* ——

Creative director and principal designer, Gillianne Griffiths is normally noted for her distinctive dark, monochromatic style; however, this three-level city dwelling marked a departure from her usual aesthetic.

While retaining the studio's dark language, it embraces a luxurious, textured design inspired by the pioneering work of Kit Kemp and her Firmdale Hotels, along with the enriched aesthetic of a London townhouse.

Trusted by her client, who bought the property unseen, Griffiths embarked on a design journey rooted in Kemp's vibrant and eclectic style.

'I wanted to infuse the space with my unique twist, starting with a foundation of black and white as predominant colours, gradually introducing rich, contrasting notes,' she says.

The transformation began at the entrance, with a new, black front door painted in Dulux 'Black' – a nod to the iconic Belgravia and Chelsea townhouse typology. Black steel arches, windows and doorways pervade the interior, marrying an industrial aesthetic with refined touches, creating an atmosphere that is both bold and elegant.

While the existing floorplan was strategically tweaked, such as transforming the ground-level powder room into a wine cellar bar with steel joinery, the true heart of the renovation lies in the primary bedroom suite. Moody and reminiscent of high-end hotels, the suite boasts a spacious walk-in robe and distinctive steel arches, adding a touch of drama to the private space.

Throughout the residence, carefully curated layers enhance the visual experience. Volker Haug Studio's lighting, the wide, white smoked parquetry timber flooring, and furniture by Studio Griffiths Architecture + Design come together harmoniously. Rich mustard velvet armchairs in the living room stand out, while homages to Kemp include custom-designed, tartan-patterned carpet in the cinema and study downstairs.

'The result is a beautiful, elegant interior,' Griffiths says.

———

The geometric lines in Henry Santoso's wire sculpture adds a layer of depth in keeping with Kit Kemp-designed hotels.

Adding another layer is one of Volker Haug Studio's recognisable Only U pendants, finished in Very Dark Bronze in the ground floor living room. It's one of several of the studio's pieces in the Balmerino Residence, each celebrating curved forms.

For designer, Volker Haug, his passion for lighting began when he was a child, fascinated by the way light works. At the age of ten, he made his first collection in a wood workshop on holiday in the Czech Republic.

'I have always been tinkering with lights as far back as I can think,' Haug says. 'It is like a mystery of how it can highlight a space.'

Later, when he was working as a hairdresser in his hometown, Stuttgart, Germany, some of his first salon clients entrusted him to craft custom lights for their homes. Lighting design and hairdressing may not seem to go hand in hand, but for Haug the two disciplines are inextricably linked.

Like cutting hair, lighting design is highly sculptural, working with shapes. Haug relished the opportunity to create long-lasting friendships with his clients.

Today, Haug has spent almost twenty years in the business he began in his garage. His works present a minimalist language of elegant lights beautifully finished and displayed.

In his own home, it's a different story. 'I can't stop finding new things. My house is full of lights,' he laughs.

"

LIGHTING IS ALWAYS VERY MAGICAL FOR ME.

—— *Volker Haug* | *Volker Haug Studio* ——

"

MY WORK IS TO FIND, NURTURE AND SHARE TALENT AND BEAUTY.

—— *Irina Rybakov* | *pépite* ——

A closer look into the rooms of the Balmerino Residence also reveals a delicate collection of ceramics; a collaboration between designer and art consultant Swee Lim and the founder and director of pépite, Irina Rybakov.

All ceramics were hand-picked to display throughout the interiors, including an effusive vase by Dawn Vachon atop the mantelpiece in the living room.

'I aim to create emotions within interiors,' Rybakov says. 'The bigger picture is that it also helps the public visualise and understand how to introduce artwork in the form of objects into their home and the impact it can have.'

The French word *pépite* translates as 'a good find' or 'a hidden gem'. It's a perfect fit for Rybakov, who founded pépite to be more than simply a showcase for handmade ceramics and sculpture. She was inspired to create a platform dedicated to uncovering fresh artists, supporting their creative expression and practice and guiding them to present their work to the wider public from her informal gallery and retail space.

'A crucial element is to identify artists that have a truly unique voice and visual language,' she says. 'And I must love every piece I show.'

As a result, she's grown her business to represent more than sixty artists. Each treasured piece is a one-off or limited-edition work and the works mostly comprise ceramics, but also glass, precious metals and artworks.

They are displayed in her ever-evolving showroom, which is not a conventional 'white cube' gallery but rather a feast for the senses, a treasure trove of creativity, beauty and visual stimulus, and the foundation for pépite's artists and the public.

The space also sparks meaningful connections for the numerous architects, designers, stylists and photographers she collaborates with and who trust her to find the right pieces to highlight their projects.

Her mission is complete once a piece has been seen, appreciated and matched with a new home, where it can create a new story and impact its owners for many years to come.

'My role is to spark collaborations that will ultimately bring more joy to spaces and everyone involved,' she says.

From the black front door through to the sculptural pendants and delicate ceramics, the Balmerino Residence is a taste of London far away from the madding crowds.

———

The deliciously bulbous forms of Dawn Vachon's *Thick Thaw* vase on the mantelpiece, from pépite.

A mix of pépite vessels and vases create handcrafted layers in the Balmerino Residence, including the Iggy & Lou Lou *Ceramic Grecian vase* on the dressing room table (bottom left) and the *Ceramic vessel* by Simone Karras on the benchtop (opposite).

FEMININE BEAUTY

STITCHED, STYLISH, CLASSIC

HAVERBRACK

—

BEATRIX ROWE

+

SUZY ESKANDER | HOUSE OWNER
SHELLEY HANNIGAN | ARTIST

"

I DO LOVE THE HANDMADE NATURE OF THINGS.

—— *Beatrix Rowe* | *designer and artist* ——

How do you inject the vibrancy and flair of a fashion stylist into a period house that feels more lacklustre than luxurious? For an answer, the house's owner, Suzy Eskander, turned to director, Beatrix Rowe, whose response was to insert contemporary elements within the traditional interior and create new layers that better reflected life, family and work.

The first layer was a functional floor plan. Rowe worked within the footprint to retain the front rooms and layout while tweaking the structure in the rear kitchen, family and dining area to improve overall flow and functionality.

New fun spaces were added: large walk-in robes, generous bathrooms and a rear studio that Eskander works from, plus beautiful gestures within the spaces for large-scale entertaining, including marble, textiles and fabrics echoing her love for fashion.

'The family has a great eye for art, and furniture too, so that's the element they can evolve and change over time,' Rowe says.

The second layer revealed the true joy of this home: high, arched French doors in steel and glass in the entrance and living areas, featuring elegant, sweeping circle motifs. The fine profile of the steel frames creates minimal sightlines, while the language is repeated throughout the house to fit the brief: contemporary, yet traditional.

'It's less frame and more glass,' Rowe says. 'And there's something about an arch that feels less jarring than other forms – they're very easy to live with.'

Rowe, also a product designer, created black steel sculptures to furnish Eskander's house, perfect complements to the rounded detail in the arched French doors.
Rowe had developed her first range on holiday a few years earlier, pulling out her notepad and starting to sketch curves, soft circles and straight lines designed to sit on a shelf or wall, in a group or on their own.

'The forms of the sculptures are open to an individual's interpretation, but to me, they read like music, and it is sort of a visual way of expressing music,' she says.

In production, every piece is sent to a local steel metalworker and returned to her for stamping and powder coating.

'I love seeing them throughout the process, seeing how the light catches them and the shadows they cast, and then the conception of an idea through to having it made,' she says.

The musical notes referenced in Beatrix Rowe's leaning steel sculptures (above) mirror the circular language of the arched steel windows in Haverbrack (opposite), adding a sense of playfulness.

"

IT'S THE SMALL, SIMPLE DETAILS THAT CAN GIVE YOU AN ELEVATED LOOK.

—— *Suzy Eskander* | *house owner* ——

When Rowe designed the space above the garage in Eskander's home, she created the quintessential flexible, optional, multipurpose room.

But with its striking wood-lined walls and aesthetic, wildly different from that of the main home, it was destined for greater things. It soon became Eskander's studio, a tucked-away, separate space where she styles, dresses and collaborates with many of the country's highest profile actors, presenters, celebrities and fashion brands through her business, Suzy Eskander Style and Aesthetic.

Eskander is a visual stylist, and the studio's back wall is often covered in lookbooks, while occupying the floor space are up to four clothes racks, holding all manner of millinery, shoes and fashion objects, delivered from around the world for her and her clients.

'It fills and gets very cluttered very quickly,' she laughs.

Her mother was a sewer, and she hand-stitched beautiful outfits for Eskander to wear to parties and balls.

'Even as a child, I spent days in the dress-up box at home,' she says.

Happily, that's never stopped. She has an innate confidence in her style and a love for small details done beautifully that relate closely to her philosophy on the intertwined relationship of fashion, design and architecture.

'The power of fashion is that our houses are reflecting the same trend of minimalism and tonal looks currently in our wardrobes. You're adding the accents and flowers but showcasing the design and element of the house,' she says.

With her accents in the studio including artist Shelley Hannigan's sublime wire dresses, there's room for creativity from every angle.

———

In her studio, Suzy Eskander holds a dress designed by Anna Antal, with Shelley Hannigan's wire *Black dress* silhouetted against the wood-lined walls.

For example, Shelley Hannigan's handcrafted translucent dresses seem to hang delicately by a thread, investigating how conventional clothing can shift into new contexts and create a new conversation about art.

Two of her pieces – *Selve-age 7* and *Anne Drysdale* – hang in Eskander's studio, at the rear of her Haverbrack home, where they are a fitting homage to the unique juncture of fashion and architecture. When installed in a domestic setting, Hannigan's dresses shift from the conventions of a wardrobe to the domain of art.

'They're quite ethereal, and each of them has its own personality,' she says.

Hannigan makes each piece by hand from fine metallic tapestry thread and copper wire, allowing the shape and design to emerge as she works.

As part of her creative process, she deliberately drops stitches and tears sections to reflect the reality of life for women in rural places.

'I'm exploring the way dresses have followed the shape of women's bodies, accentuating certain parts. Women's bodies have often been abused and then mended, so I'm expressing that too,' Hannigan says.

An accomplished painter, she returned to the comfort of knitting inspired by a photograph of her great-great-grandmother in her 'Sunday best' and the sensibilities of the Victorian and Elizabethan styles.

'It was the first art form I was taught as a five-year-old,' she says. 'There was some comfort in that, but I also wanted to nurture my creativity.'

For each of these creative women, design and fashion are inextricably intertwined with Haverbrack the most fitting expression of their collective talents.

"

IT'S A KIND OF FEMININE BEAUTY, A HUMAN QUALITY IN AN INTERIOR SPACE.

Shelley Hannigan | *artist*

SALIENT GREEN

CONNECTED, UNEXPECTED, TEXTURED

EVERGREEN HOUSE

—

ROBSON RAK ARCHITECTURE & INTERIORS

+

THOMAS LENTINI | STUDIO THOMAS LENTINI
SCOTT LEUNG | ECKERSLEY GARDEN ARCHITECTURE

"

IT WAS ABOUT CONNECTING TO THE LANDSCAPE AND MAKING THE HOUSE QUITE TRANSPARENT.

—— *Kathryn Robson* | *architect* + *Chris Rak* | *interior architect* ——

From the front door to the rear garden, the journey through this home is a rich conversation of greenery and landscape.

Partners in life, work and co-directors of Robson Rak Architecture & Interiors, Kathryn Robson and Chris Rak, have used their love of clean lines, form and natural materials to create a home in which the intention for every room was that it should be adjacent to a green space.

'We wanted to take people on a journey down the side of the house underneath a green arbour, instead of walking into the centre of the building in front,' Robson says.

The home features a central stone spine with open spaces on either side, while three-storey voids pool light into pocket courtyards. At the end of every corridor and every turn, there is a tree outside, foliage cascading down or growing upwards, amid overflowing plantings.

The basement houses a roofless courtyard containing plantings that rise two levels, meaning the tops of the trees are visible from the ground floor. Across the floor plan, outdoor spaces become part of the indoor experience.

'It makes you feel like you're connected to something bigger than the things we worry about every day,' Robson says. 'It's such a calming force.'

The internal and external floor finishes are the same, blurring the line between inside and out, while each space takes a multigenerational approach for the owners.

In signature Robson Rak style, the home contains other fun, unexpected details. The limestone walls form a gallery backdrop for the owners' art collection, instead of a sheer white canvas.

'We love texture and natural materials and layering things onto that,' Rak says.

They also created a timeless look through the furniture, which they selected together during construction.

'It's a seamless approach that has worked well for us, and it creates buildings that are just beautiful to live in,' Robson says.

————

Objects and art complement Evergreen House's freeflowing aesthetic, including Sam Michelle's *Vases, Flowers & Shapes* work and Halcyon Lake rug (top right) and two Ligne Roset's classic Togo sofas (top right and bottom).

"

I'M TRYING TO INTEGRATE AS MANY MEDIUMS AS I CAN INTO MY DESIGN LANGUAGE.

—— *Thomas Lentini* | *Studio Thomas Lentini* ——

An accomplished furniture maker, Thomas Lentini was invited to craft a commissioned piece for Robson Rak: an ambitious, 5-metre-long, twenty-two-seat dining table for the dining room.

'This was my moment to prove myself and show not only the level of design I could bring but the scale of a piece that I could produce on my own,' he says.

The table tested him on every level. The 4.4 metre lengths of timber sourced for the table came from oak trees that were 300 millimetres wide and from trees between 100 and 130 years old from a mill in New York State.

After many weeks of concepts, discussions and then execution in his workshop, the table was finally finished and sits beautifully in its place.

Lentini's first love has always been timber. He was only five when he discovered woodwork, after his father, a carpenter by trade, took him to the garage to reveal the solid timber, 3.5-metre-long sailing boat he had just built.

'He turned the light on, and it was the most beautiful thing I had ever seen,' he says.

Now, he's just as focused on evolving his work and embracing other materials, including glass, stone, steel and brass, building on the potential Robson Rak first saw in him.

'They've changed my life and given me opportunities to allow me to think at a greater scope and scale and be more bold than ever,' he says.

———

Thomas Lentini pushed the boundaries of timber craftsmanship with his twenty-two-seat dining table, below the Le Klint series pendant from Great Dane Furniture.

When it came to the Evergreen House's verdant landscaping, Robson Rak turned to landscape designer Scott Leung and his team, who transform gardens into seasonal celebrations. Leung had plenty of fertile opportunities with the site's high-massing, sunken garden elements, indoor and outdoor landscaping, and space atop the car park basement.

Working closely with Robson Rak from the start, Leung integrated a series of six tranquil 'green canvases' that present differently as you move through the house. Each has its own personality and function, depending on the time of day, from the entry garden and Virginia creepers on overhead wires to the internal courtyard and sunken gardens at the back.

Clusters of potted and raised gardens soften the heaviness of the building materiality, using the foliage and structure of plants including Japanese maples in huge cylinders, while the internal garden contains planters of mixed heights and aspects, depending on where you stand.

'Once the doors are open, the internal courtyard just feels like it's part of the house,' Leung says.

The house speaks to Leung's philosophy of allowing the plants and grasses to show their natural shapes and forms rather than resembling sculptural pieces that must be clipped and maintained. Perhaps it's a tribute to his childhood memories of hand-picking leaves off the front lawn for his dad, a keen gardener.

'We've all come from a horticultural background, so we love experimenting with plants to feel like an actual garden, with textures and a little bit of diversity,' he says.

When combined, the overall effect is of rich, layered canvases that blur inside and out, where spaces dissolve into one another and colours nourish the senses.

"

TODAY THE BIGGER PICTURE IS ABOUT GREENING THE WORLD.

Scott Leung | *Eckersley Garden Architecture*

Outdoor furniture including Fermob's metal Sixties Armchairs and Table brings the outdoors into the interior, framed with creeping greenery and lush landscaping.

SPATIAL
RESONANCE

EXPANSIVE, HABITUAL, UPLIFTING

WALDEN SHED

—

NOXON ARCHITECTURE

"

I THINK THERE'S SOMETHING ABOUT THIS PROJECT THAT IS ESPECIALLY UPLIFTING AND QUIET.

—— *Justin Noxon* | *architect* ——

When Justin Noxon, director at Noxon Architecture bought a rural, 1970s brick house to renovate for his family, it was basic and pragmatic, with potential.

'For us, it was a little bit like an idealised escape,' he says.

His vision was to expose his busy city children to a purer and simpler way of life, stripping back living to basic rituals done well. A firepit for gathering, an outdoor shower for bathing and a new project for him to create: a simple shelter shed for accommodation, separate from the 3-hectare block's main cottage.

The shelter reads as a singular, black envelope; it is made from matt corrugated steel and comprises four walls, concrete floors and one room. The room is wrapped in a structural chipboard product, and inside are a bedroom and sitting area and a small bathroom beneath stairs that lead to a mezzanine loft. Smart joinery includes a bar fridge and space to hang clothes, while a charred-timber screen pulls back to reveal spectacular rolling-landscape views.

'It's rustic and raw with a kind of durable, elemental richness, the most basic feeling of shelter,' Noxon says.

What it lacks in size it makes up for in little moments of joy and delight, from the voluminous sense of space upon entry to the dappled light that makes patterns on the floor at certain times of the day. It's something that Noxon describes as 'spatial resonance' – a depth to the space that makes it a rich experience.

'It is just a simple shed room, but I think there's something about this project that is especially uplifting and quiet,' he says.

Noxon admits he's 'a bit obsessed' with architecture for placemaking and connection, and in his shed he has created a richness in mood, light and nature.

'Even on a tiny scale, these experiences are participating in these daily kinds of rituals.'

While compact, the shelter's clever design and easy living experience prove that little things can mean a lot.

———

Justin Noxon's compact corrugated steel and chipboard shelter celebrates the basic rituals of gathering, bathing and sleeping.

FRAMING LANDSCAPES

TETHERED, RESONANT, LUXE

WOODSMITH ESTATE

—

ABE McCARTHY ARCHITECTS

+

SAM BARBER | BARBER DESIGN
JAMES NEVILLE-SMITH | HOUSE OWNER

"

THROUGH THE FRONT DOOR, CLEAR GLASS FRAMES A VIEW OF THE LANDSCAPE AS IF IT WERE A PAINTING.

—— *Abe McCarthy* | *architect* ——

At its heart, this spectacular timber home tells a story of framing views. Nestled into a paddock halfway down a hill, it faces undulating farmland that anchors the house into its rural landscape. This blends hazily into the horizon with glimpses to the coast beyond, providing a very special aspect for director, Abe McCarthy, to start from.

'It was quite staggering,' he says. 'A beautiful sight and a great opportunity.'

Working closely with his client, James Neville-Smith, he designed the home as three integrated pavilions with double-height 'loft' spaces upstairs, reflecting a Scandi sort of Euro-barn-style aesthetic, with rich timber, glass, steel and stone throughout.

The interiors were softened and grounded by Alice Villella, director of AV-ID, who injected a sense of luxury through artisanship, the materials palette, fabrics and textiles, embracing the outdoors and taking the house from day to night seamlessly.

'You feel as though you're taken into another world,' she says.

The windows and openings are carved into the architecture to face different scenes outside, while the gabled roofs create a dialogue of sun and shadow through the day.

'It's that experience of glazing opening up towards the beautiful landscape,' McCarthy says.

To achieve the house's soaring double-height spaces, McCarthy laboured over every proportion, orientation, available light, material and element. He pushed the ceiling as high as was permitted and added a steep, 40-degree pitch to the rooflines.

Bleached Australian limestone adds an earthy, textured focus, anchoring the home to the earth and picking up on the expressed metal details, giving the entire dwelling a sense of strength and endurance. The expressed steel adds weight and support, complemented by solid timber joinery and glazing looking out to the views.

'Even walking in there during construction, you could feel its uplifting quality. It just makes you feel good,' he says.

———

In his own home, James Neville-Smith has crafted a new legacy to continue the traditions of his family and their passion for timber, with soaring ceilings and dramatic landscape views.

With its Montana-shack vibe, this house is lifted to another level through
James Neville-Smith's passion for timber.

Neville-Smith is from a three-generation forestry business; he's been around timber
all his life. As a kid, he watched his family work on every element of log regeneration and
processing, taking pride in their finished products, displaying special joinery, wall lining,
benchtops or floors they had made in their own homes.

'Timber is a part of my family's DNA,' Neville-Smith says. 'We've always been proud to
showcase the products we produce at every opportunity.'

Now the sole owner of the family business, he follows tradition, with timber telling
his own story. He sourced almost all the timber and wood products used in the house
from his forestry companies, where they were grown, milled at his sawmills
and then brought to the site.

Panels of rich, oiled Tasmanian oak with a natural finish line the exterior facade.
Internally, all the timbers are also Tasmanian oak. The vaulted timber ceilings and
walls have a tinted finish, with Woodsmith's engineered oak flooring throughout stained
to create a warm, deep-walnut finish. Neville-Smith was so committed to creating clear,
uninterrupted sightlines that the lighting is cleverly concealed
within the ceiling's structural beams.

'There's not a day that goes past where we don't verbalise how much we love it,' he says.
'At night, these massive beams are lit up, showcasing the stunning vaulted timber ceilings.
Despite the scale of the space, timber makes it cosy and homely.'

"

WE PINCH OURSELVES EVERY DAY,
TO BE HONEST.

—— *James Neville-Smith* | *house owner* ——

While every opening frames an incredible landscape, the smaller, softer details are superbly
elevated by Alice Villella, including the bronze scupture by Graeme Altmann,
Returning the sound to the sea (top right and bottom).

"

WE TREAT EVERY PROJECT AS A PIECE OF LAND ART.

Sam Barber | *Barber Design*

Finally, the design of the surrounding hillside site was placed in the hands of landscape designer, Sam Barber. His early years, spent on the beach surfing, in the high country riding horses and with his hands either in the garden or on the tools, created fertile ground for a career in landscape architecture.

'My passion became about creating and experimenting with different mediums. Treating landscape architecture more like sculpture and composing a piece of art out of every project,' he says.

Working with McCarthy, he applied that thinking to Neville-Smith's farmland paddock. The challenge was that the site had already been cut and levelled ready for the build.

'How could we use the earth and mountains and shape them like a sculptor would clay?' Barber says.

His response was to soften the landscape and provide sculptural form around the entire building that also bled into the surrounding pasture, by carefully shaping and proportioning extensive earth mounds. With some as large as 45 metres long, 6 metres wide and 3 metres high, the mounds feature mass plantings of silver grass (*Miscanthus sinensis*), providing balance and subtle seasonal change.

Of the mounds, Barber says, 'They're substantial, significant forms, revealing moments of soft lines, fluid curves, deliberate glimpses of views; and combined with our mass plantings, they provide a unique rhythm that breathes in the wind.'

With the soaring timber elements and Barber's artful approach to the landscape, this house elevates simple materials to create a powerful environment that sings all the way to the coastline.

OPEN
EMBRACE

CULINARY, ELEMENTAL, SOULFUL

CUNNINGHAM RESIDENCE

—

STUDIOFOUR

+

SARAH HENRY | ARCHITECT

"

IT'S A SMALL HOUSE THAT HAD TO UNFOLD WITH THE FUNCTION OF A LARGER HOME.

—— *Annabelle Berryman and Sarah Henry* | *architects* ——

When acclaimed Australian architect Wayne Gillespie designed his first house to live in, in 1972, it was ahead of its time and laid a foundation of themes he drew on later, throughout his work.

But by the 2020s its layout was unsuitable for relaxed, contemporary living. The small kitchen had been relegated to a back room, and other spaces felt compartmentalised and experimental. This left a less-than-joyful interior for its new owner and their two children, who enjoy cooking together and embracing the outdoors.

'It had some magic to it, but this was about strengthening Gillespie's original concepts and providing a house more in tune with how the owner wanted to live,' Annabelle Berryman says, who was engaged for a full renovation along with her studiofour co-director, Sarah Henry.

Cooking took centre stage, and the kitchen was completely remodelled as the focal point of the design. It was relocated to the centre and rear of the home's key living space, allowing the family to come together with a greater connection in the new heart of the home.

The highlight is its solid American oak timber, custom-made dining table, designed by Berryman and Henry. A hybrid between an island bench, a plant bento box and a dining table, it has a central stainless-steel slot to hold utensils or for growing seasonal herbs and acts as a buffer between cooking and entertaining or studying and chatting.

'The kitchen is now established as the heart and soul of the home and encourages togetherness and gathering,' Berryman says.

At the same time, studiofour's effortless minimalist approach is brought into the interior to blur inside and out. This one large living space is flanked by floor-to-ceiling windows bookended by two small courtyards, providing sunlight and leafy aspects.

'We wanted to increase this home's connection to nature and its immersion within the landscape, to feel as though the garden was not just something to experience when outside.'

Other portals enhance connections between rooms and bring in light, including enlarged windows that were popped out to create a window seat.

Gillespie's original grey palette is honoured through the neutral 'Dark watermark' tonal paint selection, and the intent of the original staircase has been retained, but it was updated with a timber finish crafted into the treads.

'The real value to us is to provide more than just a shelter ... a home that optimises our client's health and wellbeing,' Berryman says.

Henry's love of food infuses her architectural designs and weaves its way
through her projects.

She brings food to life on finished-project photo shoots, in a tradition where she pairs the
project design with a dish she has created and prepared for the day of the shoot.

'Both design and cooking involve a series of iterations and a refining of the process to
achieve a desired outcome,' Henry says.

For the Cunningham Residence, the pairing between architect and food creates
a beautiful union with the custom, hybrid dining table and adds a new twist
on an iconic house design.

The discussion with the owner starts with finding a connection between a scenario that
might occur in the home and the overall house design, using the sensory experience of
a particular food. Colour, texture, light and form are all important aspects, with each
ingredient carefully considered and curated.

With a childhood filled with cooking and extended family gatherings,
Henry is passionate about the power of food, celebration, connection and design.
She enjoys applying the evocative layer of food as part of the design process,
recognising the crossover with her architectural work.

'Cooking brings us together to celebrate, to learn and to provide comfort.
It's a way for my family and me to be together, providing time to connect whilst
creating something together,' she says.

With cooking a huge part of the brief, for the family who lives in the Cunningham
Residence, it was a serendipitous pairing that will pay off in years to come.

"

CREATING A DISH IS IN A WAY VERY SIMILAR TO CREATING ARCHITECTURE.

— *Sarah Henry* | *architect* —

Designed by Berryman and Henry, and styled by Henry with kohlrabi and mixed salad herbs,
the American oak timber dining table is the central focus around which family life unfolds.

LIGHT RELIEF

CRISP, SHADOW PLAY, TEXTURED

THE WHITE HOUSE

—

BOWER ARCHITECTURE & INTERIORS

"

IT HAS A LOT OF LAYERS OF TEXTURE AND SHADOW PLAY AND DEPTH.

—— *Anna Dutton Lourié and Chema Bould* | *architects and interior designers* ——

When Tara and Randall Wood welcomed a third child into their family,
prompting a move for more space, they settled on a mid-century home and reached out
to Bower Architecture & Interiors.

After concluding that the existing house was dilapidated and unfit for purpose,
co-directors Anna Dutton Lourié and Chema Bould set out to create a new chapter
for the family within the compact 400-square-metre site. And made it fun, by flipping
convention and playing with space.

'This was a real exercise in massaging and shaping,' Dutton Lourié says.

The house and garden are sunny yet private, compact but approachable.
The house, over two floors, provides the family with a clean, fresh canvas on which to
layer their art and furniture.

A key to its success is Dutton Lourié's reinterpretation of the traditional rear backyard,
which has been flipped to the front, to access northern sunlight on the street side.
A smaller, intimate courtyard was created for the rear.

'Central living areas connect these two outdoor spaces, allowing one to flow to another,
joining the heart of the house with its surroundings,' she says.

Other clever moments include a gable and hipped roof on the first floor, which presents
playfully to the street while complying with strict regulations. It imbues each space with
its personality through the landscape it captures, from the window seat and
intimate kitchen to the upstairs kids' level.

'The house and garden feel both private and interwoven: the views and interactions with
outdoors bring them a sense of spaciousness,' Bould says.

As the finishing touches were applied, Tara Wood set to work styling the house,
researching textures, colours and designs with a cross between a Scandi and a
mid-century-modern aesthetic. Despite her meticulous selections, the true joy
of the house is in the way its overall design forms a beautiful backdrop
against which everything else shines.

'The angles through the sections of the house make the little things stand out.
It's beautiful,' Wood added.

———

By flipping the traditional backyard to the front, The White House optimises the
floor plan comprising 232-square-metres and site of only 400-square-metres.

White layers create shadow play, filtered light and a richness to each space, punctuated by pops of colour including a red heart work by Holly Wilmeth, *'Corazon' Mexico* (top right).

MODERN ART = I COULD + YEAH, BUT
DO THAT   YOU DIDN'T

STILL LIFE

BOTANICAL, LUSH, CURATORIAL

FOREST GLADE

—

SWEE DESIGN

+

SAM MICHELLE | ARTIST
MARITA SMITH | GALLERYSMITH
DAVID KIELY | HALCYON LAKE

"

ART AND SCULPTURE ADD STORIES AND LIFE TO AN INTERIOR.

—— *Swee Lim | designer and art consultant* ——

Art takes centre stage in this urban apartment transformation, where a singular vision emerges from a lush, forest-green palette and botanical theme.

The owners, retired empty-nesters, one of whom is an accomplished botanical artist, sought a fresh start, leaving their traditional furniture behind.

Swee Design's Swee Lim envisaged transforming the interiors into a rich, tranquil oasis using a mix of modern and vintage furniture layered with unique art and sculptural pieces. The owners, also avid readers, wanted one room to become a library, to house their extensive collection of books.

Lim's foundation in fine art history imbues her interior design projects with a distinctive curatorial flair, and she considers artisanship, ideas and custom details in conjunction with the interplay of form, texture and colour, creating interiors that tell a magical story.

It's all about the creative process, honed throughout her lifetime.

'Even as a child, I'd find things in the street and use these found objects to create art pieces. I'd wake up and paint all the furniture in my room overnight,' she laughs.

'I'm always seeking a point of difference, and then I take a layered approach, where one piece informs another, building up the story.'

Forest Glade epitomises her approach, with a Leeroy verdant-green sofa and deep green brass Jetclass Azure sideboard setting the stage. At the heart of the living space, a specially commissioned botanical artwork by artist Sam Michelle hangs above the fireplace. The unique pieces work harmoniously with contemporary and Indigenous artworks, custom-designed furniture and eclectic accessories, such as a handcrafted Sardinian vase traditionally bestowed on newlyweds.

'When it all comes together like a beautiful tapestry, you experience that moment of magic, where everything works,' Lim says.

———

Swee Lim sits on an Accanta Teacup Table from Origine at the entrance to Forest Glade, alongside other Origine furniture plus sculpture, *Stacked figure*, by Ella Bendrups from pépite.

Vessels and objects from pépite and Origine add layers of texture, alongside an elegant Zig Zag console by Barbera Design (bottom left) and rug by Halcyon Lake (bottom right), which complement the colour palette of Sam Michelle's artwork in the nearby lounge room (following page).

"

MY PRACTICE IS INSPIRED BY NATURE.

— *Sam Michelle* | *artist* —

Creating a deeply personal artwork is sometimes the result of a symbiotic collaboration, as was the case for artist Sam Michelle when she was commissioned through her gallerist Gallerysmith and Swee Design to create the botanical still-life centrepiece, *Pink Heath & Tasmanian Blue Gum*, for the Forest Glade lounge room.

It was a perfect fit. Michelle's focus on still life in nature complements one of the owners' work as a botanical artist, and she drew from a mood board given to her by Lim with detailed colours and the room's furniture.

The work includes a mix of Australian natives that harmonise with the colour range, along with the flowers from the owners' home states: the Victorian pink heath and the Tasmanian blue gum.

'That's what makes it special,' Michelle says. 'They wanted flowers that reminded them of personal aspects of their lives. Everything else works together in terms of the size, scale and this beautiful story within the painting as well.'

The piece was Michelle's largest produced at the time, and it was expertly hung by Lim above the fireplace, surrounded by the room's carefully considered furnishings.

Despite her long artistic career, Michelle's interest in still life in nature was aroused when she spotted a flower in a bouquet at a friend's wedding.

'It was a peony!' she says. 'I just fell in love, and for a while, my practice solely focused on painting peonies.'

Her passion grew to include other flowers, and she is obsessed with discovering new varieties, which she arranges in bouquets from her flower cart and greenhouse.

'Now, it's evolved into painting what I seasonally grow,' she says.
'And I love a crowded bouquet painting!'

Pink Heath & Tasmanian Blue Gum by Sam Michelle in the lounge room at Forest Glade.

As the director of the contemporary art gallery Gallerysmith, Marita Smith finds immense joy in the undiscovered talent of an artist who has a unique language yet to be realised.

When a young Sam Michelle came into her periphery, she was immediately interested in her ability to add something to the dialogue around still-life painting that felt fresh, new and different.

'I have a particular interest in representing women artists, because I believe that female artists are under-represented, undervalued and deserve to be recognised,' Smith says. When a work finds its perfect home, it's due to an incredible amount of work and faith behind the scenes. Smith knows every artist and what they do. She represents each without an end date, so they have complete support to explore their ideas unfettered, and she can help increase their visibility with a solid body of work.

'We've placed many, many works by women artists into public collections, which is an important marker of their standing. I'm very proud of that,' she says.

As well as Sam Michelle and Valerie Sparks, Gallerysmith also represents another female artist, Lori Pensini, whose diptych *Banksia Attenuata – Elixir* also resides in the lounge room.

Within it, the banksias symbolise strength and resilience, while the wattlebirds are metaphors for the ancestral spirits or guardians of women in her family.

'Like the women in your family, birds keep the bush alive by passing on to their babies the stories of where to go when things are blooming and when to hide,' Pensini says.

Her creative voice is informed by what she terms her 'language of flowers', in which she connects human qualities with botanical traits to convey personal inner strength and moral fibre.

'It's an extension of me as a child, where I spent hours and hours in the bush – the landscape spoke to me,' she says.

In the human world, she has dyslexia, which makes language and study challenging, but her art enables her to belong in a way that words cannot.

In her farm studio, surrounded by native Australian flora, Pensini is perfectly at peace.

'I find I have more integrity when I'm sitting in their world,' she says.

"

I LOVE IT WHEN THERE'S THAT BEAUTIFUL SYMPHONY OF FURNITURE AND ART AND DESIGN ... AND EVERYONE IS REACHING FOR THE HEIGHTS.

—— *Marita Smith* | *Gallerysmith* ——

Represented by Gallerysmith, Lori Pensini's diptych *Banksia Attenuata - Elixir* is a beautiful companion to the deep green brass Jetclass Azure sideboard below it.

Nearby in the study and library, objects grace a full-height bookshelf while a 100 per cent wool rug from Halcyon Lake lines the floor. A one-off creation handmade in Morocco's Atlas Mountains, the Moroccan Atlas #30 piece adds a softness and burst of colour.

At the helm of Halcyon Lake is David Kiely, who was only a child when his father introduced Australia to Berber carpet, in the 1970s and 80s. He grew up surrounded by what seemed like a million rolls of pure wool carpet and natural materials. He believes that his early exposure influenced his enduring interest.

'Our family home was a testament to our connection with Berber carpets. It wasn't just on the floors; we had Berber carpet on our walls and even on the roof,' he laughs.

Now, as the director of Halcyon Lake, the company his father founded, he brings the same sense of energy and anticipation to the work. At its core is a contemporary aesthetic deeply informed by time-honoured artisanship.

Its collections reflect the company's long-standing associations with makers around the world, in countries such as Germany, Belgium, Turkey, Morocco, Colombia and Sardinia, to name a few, where one-time collaborations have blossomed into cherished relationships.

'We primarily collaborate with small weaving workshops, many of which are family owned and set in remote regions,' Kiely says.

Each piece highlights the meticulous work of the weavers, with a focus on textural elements achieved through weaving techniques, beautiful colours and traditional patterns with a modern twist.

'We see rugs and carpets as vital in a domestic setting. They can transform a space by adding warmth, texture and softening the acoustics,' he says.

Anchored by Sam Michelle, Lori Pensini and David Kiely's rich pieces and its complementary furnishings, Forest Glade presents a series of beautifully crafted interiors tailored precisely for the couple who lives here.

"

HIS FACTORY WAS LIKE A BIG PLAYGROUND FOR ME AS A CHILD.

— *David Kiely* | *Halcyon Lake* —

UNSPOKEN DIALOGUE

AMBIENT, SPATIAL, PERCEPTIVE

TRANQUILLA HOUSE

—

SAMANTHA McKENZIE

If house owner and lighting designer Samantha McKenzie hadn't whisked her family away
to the shores of Lake Como for half a year, life could have been very different.

For one, she fell in love with Italy's ancient architecture: the solidity of its buildings,
the marble, the granite, the arches built brick by brick and the sheer spans that support
their weight so effortlessly.

And two, she was struck by the overwhelming calmness that the buildings elicited,
'delighting our senses'.

Upon returning, she combined these impressions in a brief for her personal new home,
with the elements of classical architecture interpreted in a modern way.

'It was about how the building felt, not so much what it looked like,' she says.

Over two floors connected by a gently curving staircase, the house features arches;
European oak flooring, concrete walls and ceilings; and an oculus skylight, creating a quiet
tranquillity. The spaces are modernised with splashes of colour – the green jumps
off the kitchen bench.

At the same time, she left her past life in sports marketing and launched a new design and
manufacturing business, Acustico Lighting. She specialises in high-end acoustic lighting
designed to provide ambient soundscapes in largely commercial spaces.

Naturally, her home displays several Acustico pendants and chandeliers – including the
Opera Chandelier – perfectly colour matched to her furniture.

'We've used acoustic foam, which absorbs and diffuses soundwaves; the lights lower
reverberation in a space by doing both,' she says.

Perhaps her love for creating acoustic calm in her business and home was
seeded as a child: every surface in her bedroom featured a texture, from carpet
pile to flocked wallpaper.

'I also spent my time sitting under this massive tree in the backyard, carving little shapes
out of wood. Nothing beautiful,' she laughs.

In a home where acoustics are everything, everything sounds perfect.

"

I SET OUT TO CREATE SENSORY SERENITY.

—— *Samantha McKenzie* | **house owner** ——

The musical references in Beatrix Rowe's wire art (top left and bottom right) add an unexpected layer,
along with a warm Lumi wall sconce from Articolo Lighting (top right). A slender horizontal
Archier Highline pendant recedes, and Acustico Lighting's Opera Chandelier takes centre stage,
above classic Thonet Bentwood chairs (bottom right).

TONAL POETRY

CONTRASTING, BALANCED, TRANSITIONAL

ALMA RESIDENCE

—

STUDIOFOUR

+

SUSANNA BILARDO | ENOKI

"

THE FOCUS SHIFTS FROM THE SURFACE TO THE SENSORY.

—— *Annabelle Berryman and Sarah Henry* | *architects* ——

Can a house tell a story of big emotions without resorting to interior dopamine dressing? Studiofour's co-directors, Annabelle Berryman and Sarah Henry tested the theory for a family who wished to renovate their Victorian-period home. They were engaged to preserve its strong heritage character but add a new contemporary glass pavilion at the rear.

Their response was to create a home of contrast – light and dark – drawing deeply on the rich neutral palette of its surroundings.

'A pattern language was developed to subtly tie the two architectural forms together while ensuring the contrast between the two remained strong and focused,' Berryman says.

The new section is lighter and brighter, better suited for contemporary living, with access to fresh air and garden aspects. It features a glass bridge connecting old and new that appears to float over water and opens to the kitchen, living and dining.

'These spaces are light, interactive and designed to support entertaining and times of togetherness with a stronger sense of wellbeing,' Henry says, bringing studiofour's sophisticated sense of refinement to the interior.

The design language of the new pavilion is an exercise in reduction, creating two separate architectural forms with very different sensory experiences.

'The materiality of the pavilion was derived from its structure or tectonics – for example, the concrete floor. The tone of the pavilion then informed the period spaces of the existing home; however, these materials and textures were deepened to provide darker, calming and more nurturing spaces.'

Ornate details and period features of the existing home weave together with the timber parquetry flooring, oversized pendant lighting and linen curtains and contrast with the refined minimalism in the new pavilion.

'Everything we thought about was trying to emphasise that contrast,' Berryman says.

———

Objects play with scale and proportion as the Alma Residence transitions from old to new, including the Tim handblown glass pendant lights by Bomma.

In the second bedroom and veiled in soft, delicate muslin, the Cumulus pendant illustrates the oversized pendant theme. It was conceived in 2009 as a sideline project before it took off unexpectedly to become one of Enoki's legacy designs.

'We wanted it to look like a lantern but also have the effect of a cloud-like cumulus floating structure,' says Enoki's designer and director, Susanna Bilardo.

The inherent language of the lantern lies in the way it is experienced, illustrating how special elements elevate a room with layers of storytelling. When you first see it, it draws you into the space, whether it's in a bedroom, above a dining area or alongside a sofa.

Once you're there, it doesn't overpower its space, regardless of whether it is presented solely or in a group. 'You sort of forget it's there. You embrace this beautiful glowing light, and that's what I love about it,' she says.

Its success is made more special because each muslin veil was handmade and fitted onto its timber frame by Bilardo's late mother, a skilled tailor.

'She used to sew to all hours and was so excited that we were doing something where we could use her skills,' she says. 'It was beautiful for us to work together.' That has since passed on to another Italian seamstress.

Bilardo first developed her love for interiors when she visited the Italian silk-manufacturing mill her cousin managed. She has enjoyed a rich and rewarding career ranging from furniture distribution and product design to interior and architectural design, alongside her creative family. Her husband, Judd Crush, is a graphic designer and director at Enoki.

'But I particularly love that my mother's legacy continues in each of these lanterns,' she says.

Light and dark, large and small, the Alma Residence is a home of refined constrasts that showcases a new pattern language.

"

IT'S SO DELICATE AND SO BEAUTIFUL.

— *Susanna Bilardo* | *Enoki* —

Enoki's Cumulus pendant, finished in white muslin, adds a delicate softness to the second bedroom, and is also chosen for the study and main bedroom.

Greg Wood's work, *Merri Creek*, above the fireplace (opposite) captures the tonal moodiness and
grey palette of the Alma Residence, alongside a Jardan sofa and E15 Palo floor lamp in the sitting room
(top left) and Articolo Lighting's Lumi wall sconce in the main bedroom (bottom right).

WAREHOUSE WHISPERS

ECLECTIC, PLAYFUL, QUIRKY

FABRICA

—

McMAHON AND NERLICH ARCHITECTS

+

KIM EDWARDS AND CHRIS QUIRK | HOUSE OWNERS

"

IT'S HIGHLY UNUSUAL TO HAVE A GRAND ROOF TERRACE ON SUCH A SMALL SITE IN THE INNER CITY.

— *Kate McMahon and Rob Nerlich* | *architects* —

The starting point for this project was in 2016, with a simple wish for a warehouse. When co-directors Rob Nerlich and Kate McMahon's clients found a slender site occupied by a two-bedroom Victorian cottage in a narrow back street, little did they realise it would inspire an epic seven-year journey.

'Chris and Kim decided, why don't we just start from scratch and see if we can build one?' Nerlich says.

They ended up with not only a modern interpretation of a gritty urban warehouse but also a home that delivers joy and beauty because it reflects its owners' personalities perfectly.

With the design led by McMahon and Nerlich, it's an extraordinary house. Despite its compact dimensions – 9.1 metres wide – it has enough space to breathe and even accommodates an onsite garage on the ground floor and a spectacular roof deck with a plunge pool.

Rising two floors, the home appears to be a single-storey factory renovation from the front. But upstairs, above the ground-floor bedroom, the open-plan living and dining level is akin to a gutted factory, with a soaring, exposed-timber-framed roof, and sunlight flooding in from three sides.

'This is the big warehouse moment,' McMahon says. 'With massive windows, extraordinary natural light and those brick walls.'

Comprising concrete floors, finely executed steel windows and clever brick veneers, the materiality speaks to the raw and robust nature of warehousing. But it is softened with sweeping curves, two spiral staircases and smaller gestures like rounded benchtops, joinery and mirrors, with the owners' elegant lighting accenting the architecture.

However, the best is saved for last. In a feat of structural engineering, the square-shaped plunge pool drops into the third-level roof deck. Anchored by huge concrete piers that run down through the ground, the pool enjoys sweeping views of urban life while being surrounded by landscaped gardens.

It was indeed a fortuitous day when a shortcut down a tight street, thanks to a dumpster blocking the road, first revealed the slender site to Kim Edwards, followed by an auction board propped up at the front of its narrow Victorian cottage.

'We bought the damn thing, and off we went,' her partner, Chris Quirk, laughs.

Seven years later, their dream warehouse was complete, a perfect marriage of seemingly unlikely passions. Quirk's retail strategy expertise meets Edwards's four-decade career as a hair and makeup artist and her obsession with fashion, colour and materials. 'I just see things differently,' Edwards says. 'To me, it all flows – fashion, styling hair, makeup artistry, interiors.'

The interior is layered with textiles, ceramics by emerging artists, Spanish tiles they love and plants they've named, creating a Spanish delight warehouse with a New York vibe that always feels like it's on holiday.

'We don't need to go away for the weekend. We just go upstairs,' Quirk jokes.

From top to bottom, lighting is the ultimate language. 'It's the sexiness of housing,' he says. They've spent many years collecting lamps, pendants, sconces and different types of lights like others collect art.

A notable mention is the large surgeon's light above the staircase, lending a sculptural aspect and presence to the room as part of the space.

There is also different lighting in every room, down to small brass bracket candleholders.

'We just love it. We don't have a huge amount of artwork, but a lot of lights,' Quirk says.

'The opportunity to give back to Australian artists is something special too,' Edwards adds.

What a way to live, immersed in space and light in the inner city.

"

EVERYTHING'S BEAUTIFUL. YOU WOULDN'T EXPECT IT TO WORK TOGETHER, BUT IT DOES.

—— *Kim Edwards and Chris Quirk* | *house owners* ——

———

Chris Quirk (left) and Kim Edwards at the entrance to their first floor living and dining space, next to a 500 millimetre aged brass surgeon light by Lost Profile Studio.

Quirkiness abounds at Fabrica, translating as factory in Spanish, with Kim Edwards relaxing on the rooftop deck (bottom left) and whimsical details including Lucy Vanstone's birds, *empty nesters*, on the dining table and vessels by Tantri Mustika in the curving joinery niche (opposite).

TRANSCENDING BOUNDARIES

LIBERTINE, SANCTUARY, ENGAGING

CANALLY MANSION

—

HECKER GUTHRIE

+

LAUREN JOFFE | CERAMIC ARTIST
GREG WOOD | ARTIST

"

WE WANTED IT TO FEEL LIKE IT HAD ITS OWN PERSONALITY.

Hamish Guthrie | *interior designer*

How do you take the stately history of a grand townhouse and the less-than-beautiful additions of its recent past and transform both into one beautiful experience for its owners?

For Hamish Guthrie, co-director of Hecker Guthrie, the starting point is always site and context. However, even the front door of this townhouse, which was originally one-quarter of a large, late-nineteenth-century mansion designed by Joseph Reed in 1864, opened straight into a slightly awkward 1970s addition. It felt immediately dark, pokey and uninspiring.

'The unique aspect of the brief was that just two people were living in what was quite a significant space,' Guthrie says. 'How do we ensure each room of the house is engaged and activated?'

With his requisite approach and sensibility to his craft, he wanted to celebrate the grand remnants and reverse engineer the rest, making sure every room – especially the most impressive – was put to use with greater liberty, given the couple were keen to explore more contemporary applications for each space.

The 1970s addition became an opportunity for a new black insertion, with strong steel gestures and a central void, and a staircase that opens up the townhouse over two levels. Beyond, the kitchen was flipped with the original, secluded dining room. Rather than a traditional space, the kitchen appears 'almost as though you have furnished the room with a series of objects and pieces of furniture', according to Guthrie.

Upstairs, the laundry and bathroom utility spaces were originally pushed away to the side but are now given greater prominence. The second bedroom was transformed into the main ensuite, while, utilising the full height of one of the grandest rooms in the house, the main bedroom embodies a dark, moody aesthetic embellished with a mezzanine level, exposed rafters and further sculptural steel work.

Another celebration is a new hybrid space crafted from one of the original 1970s additions. Connecting to the kitchen, it is referred to as the 'morning room', because it floods with natural sunlight at that time of the day.

'Given we weren't bound by the true historical nature of that space, we could take more and more liberties with our design approach while still being respectful,' he says.

By night, it becomes a drinks or library space, with a built-in yellow bar with small croissant joinery handles hidden behind custom joinery, and spills seamlessly onto the adjacent courtyard.

'It's not a traditional dining room, and we have dealt with the furniture in a slightly more informal way so that it's more functional but ambiguous,' he says.

Colour is also used subtly through objects, joinery and freestanding elements, as well as in specific spaces, to imbue emotion, such as the neutral, green tones of the main bedroom.

'It's the ultimate sanctuary,' Guthrie says.

Hamish Guthrie (above) stands in a high-arched doorway, where beautiful details include a red travertine
Mario Bellini dining table and armchairs by Botolo and Ginestra Nuda (opposite, top left), and clever
design insertions including a yellow cabinet that conceals a drinks servery (opposite, top right).

Engaging and activating the rooms are several pieces by ceramic artist Lauren Joffe, such as her large, black-and-white stoneware piece *Heartlines*.

She also designed a jewellery-like light fitting for the powder room, in consultation with Hecker Guthrie, and other small objects on display; the home's owner is a supportive friend.

'I've known the house owner since I was twelve, and when I started my artistic journey he came to every show and started collecting my work, even from the crappiest little thing!' she laughs.

For Joffe, that's the point.

'I'm happy seeing my work in a gallery space, but these are pieces that are meant to be lived with,' she says. 'I think it does transcend boundaries.'

Her journey to ceramics was preceded by a law degree, fine art gold- and silversmithing, and contemporary object- and jewellery-making.

'Those tiny little objects just weren't doing it for me,' she laughs. 'With clay, I can go bigger. I can make the forms I feel that I need to make.'

In her work, Joffe creates small and large vessels with simple forms and monochromatic colours, reflecting her rich experiences and influence of place. She was born in Cape Town, emigrated to Australia as a young child and grew up surrounded by Japanese art and antiques, as her mother worked in a Japanese art gallery.

For example, she has a mentor who can see Africa in her work, with the choice of colours, texture and overall mood and atmosphere.

'I think this all manifested its way into my artistic expression, and I can see it in the forms and in the surface itself,' she says.

"

I'M HAPPY SEEING MY WORK IN A GALLERY SPACE, BUT THESE ARE PIECES THAT ARE MEANT TO BE LIVED WITH.

—— *Lauren Joffe* | *ceramic artist* ——

Lauren Joffe fulfills her art practice using clay, including her *Heartlines* vessel (on floor) and *'Omar' bird sculpture (medium)* (on table) below the Moon 120 light pendant by Davide Groppi.

"

I OBSCURE THE FORM AND USE VERY SUBTLE TONAL SHIFTS TO CREATE AN IMPRESSION.

—— *Greg Wood* | *artist* ——

There's one more detail in perfect keeping with the muted palette in the kitchen; Greg Wood's *V15 Eternal Shift* work perched on the mantelpiece.

To experience a Greg Wood painting is to be immersed in a dream state. Tonal palettes wash over suggested landscapes, leaving interpretation wide open rather than prescriptive and literal.

'I feel my paintings take you somewhere you've been,' Wood explains. 'You can't put your finger on where, but you feel it.'

A painter since the 1990s, Wood spent a decade collaborating with Sarah Fletcher from 2011, amongst others. He is currently represented in Melbourne, central Victoria and internationally, and more recently works with Otomys on a variety of significant projects. Little has changed; he produces a body of work in one go, creating up to thirty pieces per collection.

Once the body of work leaves the studio and eventually separates, the individual pieces take on new meaning, depending on their environment, whether it be a gallery, commercial space or house.

'Its voice becomes its own story, rather than the whole body as a narrative,' he says.

'I often hear from people that the more they look at it and at different times of the day, the more they see new things in it. That's quite nice to hear.'

Showcasing new and older works, Canally Mansion imbues a worldliness that adds to its libertine nature, but it's still a lot of fun too.

———

A small Greg Wood work, *V15 Internal Shift*, sits atop the mantelpiece in the kitchen, its hues and tones a perfect match for the moody colour palette and subtle white tube Miss 1 pendant by Davide Groppi.

CRAFTED REVERIE

VIVID, EXPRESSIVE, MAGICAL

KALEIDOSCOPE

—

SWEE DESIGN

+

DAVID RAY | CERAMICIST
ANA HOLSCHNEIDER | CARALARGA
VALERIE SPARKS | ARTIST
PETER D COLE | ARTIST
SEE YEN FOO | APATO
LOUIS GRANT | GLASS ARTIST

"

THIS IS MORE THAN A HOME; IT'S A CELEBRATION OF CREATIVITY AND ARTISTRY.

—— *Swee Lim* | *designer and art consultant* ——

Classic yet contemporary, refined yet quirky, the Kaleidoscope home is a testament to the imaginative spirit and creative synergy that can arise when diverse art forms, design and cultural influences merge. Director of Swee Design, Swee Lim's brief was to 'create a sophisticated and joyful haven for adventurous art-loving clients', and she achieved it with delightful moments of whimsy and playfulness.

Throughout the home, generous spaces are furnished with highly considered works. In the living room, a striking handcrafted textile by Caralarga, from Mexico, reimagines traditional tapestry with its innovative, three-dimensional, sculptural design. In the hallway, Louis Grant's playful geometric glass works interact beautifully with the sculptural DenHolm console.

'The sunlight streaming through the towering 4-metre-high pivot door transforms each glass piece into radiant miniature jewels,' Lim says.

In the dining room, beautiful proportions and balance are paired with the organic forms of the Bloom floor lamp by Joanne Odisho, which resembles a flower, and *Christmas Tree*, a brass sculpture by Peter D Cole. Finally, special furniture pieces, including the elegant minimalist form of the Nagare chair, are juxtaposed with intricate, humorous trophies by ceramic artist David Ray.

'It creates an incredibly unique and inspiring space for its inhabitants,' Lim says.

———

From the open plan kitchen and living into the dining room, double doors reveal a beautiful freestanding floor lamp, Bloom, by Joanne Odisho made of American oak, eggshell and handblown glass.

"

I LIKE THAT IDEA OF BEING CONNECTED WITH THE MATERIAL AND THE CONVERSATION I HAVE WITH MYSELF WHILE MAKING IT.

—— *David Ray* | *ceramicist* ——

Just beyond, the open plan kitchen and living room reveals two incredibly detailed works by ceramicist David Ray - *Riot Cop* and vase, *Cut Up*.

Both rich in technique, tactility and form, they explore themes of preciousness, privilege and storytelling, among others. Represented by Fletcher Arts, Ray especially enjoys the utility of clay objects in narratives of vessels, from ancient Egypt and Greece to more recent rituals of Grandma's tea set brought out of the cupboard on special occasions.

Ray is a leading ceramic artist known for his wild, flamboyant work embellished with exquisite details and neo-Baroque influences as evidence of his 'hand at work'. His first solo exhibition, in the mid-1990s, was described as 'Wedgewood on acid'. He was nicknamed the Duke of Dirt, an affectionate homage from ceramicist and potter Gerry Wedd for his unique view on clay.

'There's always a lot going on,' he laughs. 'Once you strip down all the surfaces and take all that away, you're just left with dirt ... With each piece, I just start from scratch and see how it evolves.'

Riot Cop is one of his most popular pieces, and is the only work he produces in a small batch. He made one, which turned into 200 castings to sell, inspired by artist Richard Stringer and his bee designs.

The process allowed Ray to explore another theme – namely, community loss through mass production in the Industrial Revolution – but soon he began to see his little earthenware and gold police figures popping up in homes, on benches, next to front doors and on walls, serving as protectors and guardians.

"

THESE ARE TEXTILE PIECES MADE WITH NATURAL FIBRES.

—— *Ana Holschneider* | *Caralarga* ——

Opposite in the living room, the Kaleidoscope house twists to reveal an extraordinary piece by Caralarga, *Son Chiapaneco*.

It's made from raw cotton thread, the primary component in many everyday items, and when in Caralarga's hands, something magical happens.

'Our creative work is very spontaneous; each new project or collection opens the door to the multiple possibilities that are presented to us along the way, making it exciting and inspiring,' says Ana Holschneider, founder and creative director.

Each piece is unique from form to finish, designed by experimenting and subjecting the work to trial and error, and handmade by people with special personal stories seeking to reinterpret and transform motifs from their Mexican nature and culture.

The company collaborates with local weavers and artisan communities from its base in Querétaro, Mexico, to create sublime textile works by transforming and enhancing the qualities of the thread.

'This has been our main material and source of inspiration from day one,' she says.

As the works are appreciated and recognised in a growing number of countries and cultures, where people can see and enjoy them, a new form of dialogue arises.

'It's exciting that people value handmade work and the crafts made in Querétaro. Their minimalist essence makes them easy to coexist with other pieces of very diverse materials and styles,' Holschneider says.

When inhabiting a residential interior, as her *Son Chiapaneco* tapestry does, the works take on new meaning. Caralarga is the ultimate upcycler, re-using remnants it generated or sourcing natural, local, environmentally friendly materials to create something that is far from disposable.

'It will be part of a context and will last over time. That's what marks our pieces as timeless: they are here to stay,' she says.

Caralarga's beautiful tapestry is in good company with the eclectic *Chimphead bust vase* by Lisa Roet (on table) and Dean Bowen's *Young echidna with perching kookaburra (three leaves)* (on shelf).

THE FRENCH CAT · *Rachael McKenna*

ESCHER X NENDO
Between
Two
Worlds

VOGUE LIVING COUNTRY, CITY, COAST

Resident Dog

The nearby dining room features a striking work by Valerie Sparks,
Le Vol 1 Allusion & Illusion.

Inspired by the European fantasy of the exotic, it features birds from the collections of
various natural history museums.

It enables the homeowner to live immersed in an environment with grand mythical themes
and creates a new dialogue between the architecture of the room and the fictitious
imaginary spaces of the work.

'I really want to encourage people to just exist for a while in the process of looking,
where they get lost in the sense of sight,' Sparks says. 'And the sense that we can't control
everything: things always fall beyond our ability to pin down.'

At first glance, Sparks's art appears ethereal, almost too real.

That's precisely the point. 'I am a bit of a dreamer,' she says. 'I just really love the
bizarreness of creating these highly constructed environments.'

Upon closer inspection, her works are not just detailed but hyper-detailed, with laser-cut
perfection. Often, she features birds and layers of landscape in misty, grey and blue hues
that seem as though they're within a real space but at the same time are surreal.

'That's what I aim for. You're hovering in that liminal kind of space between
real and unreal,' she says.

Her unique art practice emerged after she explored 18th- and 19th-century wallpapers.
She'd picked up a book about a French scenic wallpaper from the 1860s and began to look
at other wallpaper variations, including scenes of promenades in Italy, buildings in France,
and a battle scene from the 1830 French Revolution which covered an entire room.

'They just blew my mind,' she laughs.

She decided to make her own, cautiously transitioning to an art career at thirty-nine years
old; she is now represented by Gallerysmith. She creates each piece from hundreds of
landscape images, which she imports and layers, image by image. She uses them to build
a panorama and then a final photographic form, often installed in full-height wallpaper
format lining whole rooms.

"

I WANT PEOPLE TO HOVER BETWEEN THE
IMAGINARY AND THE ACTUAL.

—— *Valerie Sparks* | *artist* ——

"

IT'S A CONTINUAL PROCESS OF PLAY.

—— *Peter D Cole* | *artist* ——

In the dining room sits a collection of objects including Peter D Cole's
Christmas Tree sculpture.

Each shape in the piece utilises geometry – a circle, triangle or square – represented in
primary colours as well as brass. By enlarging, minimising, lengthening and solidifying each
shape on a three-dimensional scale, he creates different meanings and interpretations.

'It's just the way I work. You play with the object and you play with the space,' Cole says.

His love for modernism harks back to his childhood, spent in the architect-designed home
his parents built, which included a 20-metre-long, north-facing wall of glass.

'It was glass with several coloured doors the whole way along, and the light pouring in
from the north was incredible. We also had a carport that had a walled screen made up of
panels of twelve different colours,' he says.

Represented by Fletcher Arts, Cole's colourful upbringing is a clear influence on his
sculptures and his recent preoccupation with the Bauhaus movement.

Sometimes, letters and words appear in his work that project a political message, and
often his works read from left to right: 'There's a lot of linear aspects to the work, and the
lines become a way of holding the form in a particular position,' he says.

While he doesn't like to keep old pieces lying around in the studio adjoining his home –
'too distracting' – his home is a rich juxtaposition of objects, Marc Newson and
Mario Bellini furniture, centuries-old pieces, plus art and sculpture, including work by his
wife and son, both of whom are also artists.

He continually moves things around, mixing the layers of history, time and patina:
'I think it becomes more of a tension. Just having something of all the one genre
doesn't become a living space,' he says.

———

Peter D Cole's brass *Christmas Tree* sculpture sits atop a Jetclass Azure sideboard with brass accents,
in perfect keeping with Swee Design's interior palette.

"

THE FINAL DETAILING AND JOINERY ARE ALL TRADITIONALLY HANDMADE.

See Yen Foo | *Apato*

In a quieter moment and in a departure from colour, the living room features Masayuki Nagare's innovative Nagare Chair, represented by Apato. Constructed from high-quality walnut wood with advanced woodworking techniques, the chair was revolutionary at the time he designed it, in 2005, as his first venture into furniture-making with manufacturer CondeHouse.

Today, its lack of conventional lines and play of light and shadow are timeless. They relate beautifully to David Ray's delightful, lopsided trophies on the mantelpiece.

For more than a decade, director See Yen Foo has celebrated and championed the timeless craft of Japanese design through his business, Apato. He represents eight core Japanese brands, working with high-profile designers including Naoto Fukasawa and Motomi Kawakami and emerging talents such as nendo and Inoda + Sveje.

'Most of our brands have been established for more than sixty years and are very well known in Japan,' Foo says. 'They enjoy seeing their work around the world in different settings.'

While Apato is best known for its focus on chairs, it takes the same meticulous approach to its entire collection. Each piece is created, designed and made in Japan by craftspeople passionate about timberwork. They typically use a mix of ancient techniques and innovative Japanese design, with the final touches and details finished by hand.

Fortuitously, Japanese design is gaining more traction in Australia. The aesthetic shares similarities with Scandinavian design: a well-detailed and well-made approach to shapes and proportions.

'Everything's very toned down but yet modern and elegant,' Foo says, 'and ultimately comfortable in our homes.'

Masayuki Nagare's Nagare Chair sits below ceramicist David Ray's *Champions (Trophy Series)*, which riffs on traditions of pride and winning.

There's a final surprise in the hallway. Two of glass artist, Louis Grant's pieces, titled *I like to feel my bones when they crash into my heart* and *I'm trying to keep away from you*, reflect his material language perched atop DenHolm's console.

'There's this sublime aspect to the work,' Grant says. 'I like to make the glass sometimes not look like glass, but like resin or jelly.'

Ever since he was introduced to the art of glass, as an eighteen-year-old, Louis Grant has had a clear, creative affinity with the material that is perfectly aligned with his experience as a queer young man.

'It's another state of being, not liquid and not solid, but amorphous and chemically super interesting,' he says.

With glass as his primary medium, he focuses on kiln forming, in which he fuses flat sheets cut into different shapes and arrangements. He also uses cold working, in which he cuts, grinds and polishes the glass after it's been heated. He embraces the highly technical and process-driven nature of the practice as he experiments with scale, form, composition, tone and texture.

He may leave scratches in the glass or introduce materials such as cement or terrazzo. When installing or exhibiting his work, he sometimes paints the walls different colours, interested in creating tension and balance, or softness or harshness.

'I play with that. A lot of the works use pastel colours, and some are more modular, like building blocks, so you can move them around,' he says.

Represented by Fletcher Arts, Grant makes his pieces in his world-class glasswork studio, partnering with others – 'glass is a team sport' – and names them after lyrics in pop songs.

'But it's really all about the material,' he laughs.

With its rich riot of work – large and small – that creates such a strong impact, the Kaleidoscope home is a place for colour, the unconventional and the unexpected wrapped up with a good dose of whimsy.

"

GLASS IS NON-BINARY, NEITHER THIS NOR THAT.

—— *Louis Grant* | *glass artist* ——

Eye-catching glass artwork by Louis Grant titled *I like to feel my bones when they crash into my heart* and *I'm trying to keep away from you* sits below a limestone wall piece by Mitch Fong for DenHolm titled *Daisy*.

DOWN TO EARTH

INGRAINED, SMOOTH, INTIMATE

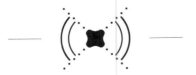

RIVER HOUSE

—

BEATRIX ROWE

"

THE HOUSE WAS A LOVELY WEATHERBOARD HOMESTEAD.

—— *Beatrix Rowe* | *designer and artist* ——

Sometimes, a place we love gets under our skin. For director, Beatrix Rowe, that place was the town where she grew up: an iconic regional port with paddle steamers, old timber wharves and the winding, gum-lined Murray River.

When the opportunity arose to revive one of the town's renowned homesteads, with river frontage and prize-winning gardens on 4 hectares, she was overjoyed.

The home was bought by two brothers to share with their families as a holiday house. Its existing U-shape was ideal to establish two wings, which required full interior refits, including moving internal walls to achieve an optimum layout and function. Solid walls were intentionally retained, as were most of the window and door openings, while the windows and doors themselves were replaced with steel and glass, enhancing the connection to the grounds, garden and view of the river.

'We wanted to balance with the feeling of intimacy and containment that the existing home had,' Rowe says.

Internally, the kitchen and bathrooms extend the language of the homestead, its weatherboard cladding and its connection to the water, through beautifully milled timber joinery that culminates in a rear deck structure reminiscent of the historic paddle steamers of the port town.

One of the owners, Rob Morton, brought his skilful joinery to the project. Their meticulous approach saw them hand-select and mill each piece of timber, including some for a cabinet of Tasmanian blackwood salvaged from a riverbank on a private property. Rowe designed the cabinet, which Morton finished by adding timber handles: a perfect partnership.

'They are extraordinary pieces of timber, with such history and stories behind them,' Rowe says.

In the bathroom, glossy tiles glisten like sunlight dancing on water, while travertine stone vanities echo the earth, reflecting Rowe's childhood.

'Having stepped in the mud and seen the layers of the banks on the river, I feel like the travertine speaks to that earthiness,' she says.

Now, the River House is ready to bring more joy not only to the two families and their friends but to future generations as well.

The River House showcases a unique partnership between Beatrix Rowe and house owner, Rob Morton, dovetailing their skills to craft bespoke joinery, including cabinets (top right) and beautiful shelving units shown alongside artwork by Jimmy Donegan (top left and bottom right).

SPIRITED SPEAKING

ECLECTIC, CALMING, ELEVATING

SACKVILLE LOFT

—

SHARON PATSIOTIS

"

IT HAS THIS AMAZING PRESENCE ABOUT IT INSIDE AND OUT.

Sharon Patsiotis | *house owner*

Sharon Patsiotis couldn't resist the old post office: a freestanding, two-storey Victorian building in the centre of a regional town. Built in 1881, it was perfectly straight up and down, filled with natural light, beautiful architectural details and soaring ceilings.

'At one point, downstairs was used as the telecommunications hub,' Patsiotis says. 'It's the standout building here.'

This history, her memories of the area as a teenager and its sudden appearance on the property market made it irresistible for her to buy it and make it her own.

She embarked on a sympathetic renovation to celebrate the old with cosmetic rather than structural change. The downstairs chambers transitioned into separate commercial spaces, while upstairs the old offices became Patsiotis's apartment, with three bedrooms, two bathrooms and a new kitchen.

Now, it resembles a New York loft with a museum feel. A calm, white palette with lime-washed floorboards showcases tall archways, doorframe panels and restored fireplaces.

But it's Patsiotis's collection of artworks, antiques, taxidermy and knick-knacks that gives each room an eclecticism that beautifully straddles past and present, yesteryear and future.

'You could well imagine all sorts of people roaming around the town a long time ago, so we wanted to honour that,' she says.

As the founder of Hale Mercantile Co., she has sourced each piece lovingly, taken from the luxury linen label, brought back from overseas travels or simply collected locally. Each room features Hale fabrics and linens, which bring a softness and relaxed aesthetic in keeping with the building's coastal location.

'That's why Hale works so well,' she says. 'Things drape and fall, and you can't be too contemporary, because it's too crisp and sharp for a space like this.'

A taxidermy kudu, white peacock, fox, rabbit and various birds, all sourced sustainably, feature along with other touches including a Vox Populi wire lamp shaped like a ship, which she carried with her on a flight home from Paris. Nearby, shells collected from the beach decorate porcelain dishes.

The final nod of eclecticism belongs to the white peacock, which belonged to a staff member's partner, a taxidermist, and hangs from the wall in her bedroom. 'They had it in their home and decided they didn't want it, so I put my hand up,' she laughs.

It's a space rich with objects and art that shouldn't work together, but do, elevating the old post office to an eclectic home full of voices.

Founder of Hale Mercantile Co., Sharon Patsiotis enlivens her old post office home with her eclectic, layered style.

Sharon Patsiotis commissioned artist Harley Manifold to paint a landscape for her in 2017 (opposite), while most rooms contain a taxidermy creature (all sourced sustainably), and collected objects.

ENGLISH SENSIBILITIES

HANDMADE, TRADITIONAL, EARTHY

PIMLICO TERRACE

—

HECKER GUTHRIE

+

BEN MAZEY | ARTIST

"

WE EXPLORED THE IDEA OF REINSTATING THE STABLE, TO CREATE A TRADITIONAL ALMOST COURTYARD ENVIRONMENT WITHIN.

—— *Paul Hecker* | *interior designer* ——

For this family of four, home is deeply rooted in their English heritage. So when the opportunity arose to sell their contemporary digs and return to their history in a beautiful double-storey Victorian terrace, they leapt to the challenge.

With the trappings of Victorian architecture, the property is a generous but narrow terrace, facing a beautiful park to the front and with the original horse stables at the rear backing onto a bluestone-cobbled laneway. The house had an unappealing, leaking box renovation on the back, prompting Hecker Guthrie co-director Paul Hecker to consider better ways for a busy family to live within a terrace configuration.

'We explored this idea of park and reinstating the idea of stable, to create a traditional, almost courtyard environment,' Hecker says.

At the front, the grand four rooms upstairs and downstairs were retained, and the bones of the house were respected rather than stripped. The spaces were enriched and made moodier, to celebrate the language of an English house.

The leaking box at the back had to go, and it was replaced by a soaring brick living space with a pitched roof, extending the house beautifully into the garden and opening the interior with a summery, light-filled aesthetic. Just beyond, the stables became a self-contained living space with a kitchenette, bathroom and bedroom, largely used by the family's teenage boys and their friends.

'We made it out of brick rather than using contemporary materials, knowing that, over time, it will weather and patina in a positive way,' he says.

The house also echoes his design approach: 'Do it once, do it well, and it's there for a long time.' Working with the old architecture rather than against it meant that traditional materials were specified – brick, slate, stone and solid timber – and traditional approaches to construction were encouraged.

The builders and subcontractors applied this artisan approach to the building process, going beyond their traditional scopes to produce a home that embraces the handmade. The kitchen bar is a wonderful example, that through the commitment of the builder, became a piece of fine joinery.

The interiors feel seamless, connected by earthy-green colours that work well and are easy to live with.

Now, the owners have a home that truly speaks to their English tradition through its Victorian architecture.

'We had a client who was willing to live with the idiosyncrasies of a Victorian house and embraced what that looked like and what that meant,' Hecker says.

When it came to furnishing the walls, the owners had someone in mind. They were attracted to artist Ben Mazey, whose work they had been introduced to when he held his first exhibition at an art gallery. After years of work in fashion and design around the world, Mazey leaned into ceramics during the pandemic, moulding clay objects to decorate his apartment.

'I think the ceramics is just me doing something purely on my terms. And I'm really selfish, essentially,' he laughs.

Relishing his creativity, he found some success at his exhibition, where the owners commissioned him to create a piece for their entrance.

The work *Black Line Flag Crayon Diptych* could reference winter and the trees in the park opposite the house, with one rogue piece glazed white. 'It's kind of a cloud in an abstract sense,' Mazey says.

The black line, drawn freehand through each flag, might also reference how we all start somewhere and either have smooth sailing or bumpy roads as we travel through life.

Ultimately, he's reticent to describe his work prescriptively, appreciating the simplicity and calmness of his pieces without needing a clear reference. 'It becomes a chameleon, depending on the home it's in. And I'm proud of that,' he says.

His work also expresses his childhood interest in maths and repetition, which form the foundation of his practice. It triggers summer holiday memories of catching ferries that were flying flags, too.

'Depending on which way the flag stopped, it looked completely different, because it was blowing in the wind, which is that repetition,' he says.

In the studio, he makes a shape, or flag, in clay and manipulates it a little, and then a little more, turning the small slabs into a sequence.

'They're like modular Lego bricks, and then they come together to form something more than the sum of its parts,' he says.

The piece, while abstract, is beautifully suited to the English lines of the house and lifts the entrance to create intrigue and spark curiosity.

"

THE CHAMELEON NATURE IS REALLY STRONG.

—— *Ben Mazey* | *artist* ——

——

Ben Mazey's ceramic work, *Black Line Flag Crayon Diptych*, at the entrance to Pimlico Terrace, plays with line and form above Ilse Crawford's Settle bench and existing chequered floors.

Hecker Guthrie's custom-designed joinery with round finger pulls feature throughout, alongside details including a Le Klint series floor lamp from Great Dane Furniture and rug by Halcyon Lake in the dressing room (opposite) and a Volker Haug Studio wall light in the main bedroom ensuite (bottom left).

URBAN OASIS

COLLABORATIVE, HOLISTIC, SEAMLESS

HIDDEN HOUSE

—

STUDIO MKN AND ELIZA BLAIR ARCHITECTURE

+

TIM PERKINS | GEORGE FETHERS & CO.

"

COLLABORATION ENSURES BOTH THE INTERNAL AND EXTERNAL DESIGN ASPECTS ARE SEAMLESSLY INTEGRATED.

—— *Meredith Nettleton* | *interior designer* + *Eliza Blair* | *architect* ——

From its picture-book Victorian facade to its graceful heritage proportions, this house, built in 1888, had all the hallmarks of a great period home when a young couple bought it in 2010, drawn to its spacious, sloping gardens and sleepy location at the end of a no-through street.

By 2019, the addition of two children had squeezed the dimensions, and a rare opportunity arose for interior designer Meredith Nettleton and architect Eliza Blair to dovetail their creative energies into renovating the house while exploring some bold ideas.

'We once worked together in a large practice,' Blair says. 'We then went out on our own separately but joined forces on this one, knowing it would be an enjoyable process. It's not only a lot more fun working with someone else, but the outcomes are a lot more holistic.'

Blair's initial thoughts on siting and massing highlighted the design opportunity to extend out behind the formal front rooms of the house, rather than building up, and resulted in a new, long, linear pavilion immersed in the garden.

Occupying former garden space and stepping down the sloping block, it incorporates a kitchen, dining and living zone and ends with a full-width, full-height facade of custom-made, pivoting, timber slat screens, which shield the pavilion from the western sun and create privacy when needed. It's a clever use of space, the structure stretching into its site and culminating in a living area that seemingly 'floats in amongst the garden'. Tucked neatly in the back of the site is a separate studio surrounded by trees.

'Our client was willing to make some quite bold decisions and didn't shy away from using expressive modern materials such as concrete, steel and black timber cladding,' Nettleton says.

The slat screens operate perfectly and complement other strong elements of the house, such as the substantial natural stone island bench, almost like a sculptural artwork, steel accents and slimline sliding doors. The whole is softened by strategically placed skylights as well as engineered oak floors by George Fethers & Co.

While respecting the original architecture, the renovation has created a house that exudes comfort and space by blending old and new.

For Nettleton and Blair, the project further cemented their professional relationship. They now collaborate exclusively and trust each other implicitly. Their projects are seamless reflections of their meticulous marriage of architecture and interiors – with space for creativity and fun in between.

———

Meredith Nettleton and Eliza Blair enjoy the challenge of looking at things from different angles, resulting in strategic skylights and a long, stretched kitchen that hosts a dining table and chairs from Great Dane Furniture.

In particular, Blair specified George Fethers & Co.'s Ottó XVI Flint flooring throughout the house: a grey European oak with taupe hues and a matt lacquer finish. At 240 millimetres, the planks are wider than the industry standard, creating an added sense of space and luxury.

'It's beautiful. I'm very much inspired by the creatives we work with, and we relish the thought of our products adding to the ambience of a beautiful family home and being enjoyed for generations,' managing director, Tim Perkins says.

When an interiors business can trace its heritage back four generations, to 1865, it's little surprise that a language of longevity and quality is deeply embedded within its products.

Fourth-generation family member Tim Perkins owns the business with his father's cousin, but it was his great-grandfather who founded the legacy, starting work there in the early 1900s as an office boy. The rest, as they say, is history, with the company having survived two depressions, two World Wars and a diversified interest in timber, glass and now solar.

'Today, I consider myself a custodian rather than an owner,' Perkins says. 'I'm very proud to be part of the transition from net carbon emitters to carbon-neutral energy consumers.'

Under foot, the flooring feels comfortable and grounds Hidden House perfectly into its garden; another nuanced layer in its story.

"

IT'S INSPIRING TO BE INVOLVED IN BUILDING BEAUTIFUL THINGS.

—— *Tim Perkins* | *George Fethers & Co.* ——

Beautiful pops of colour punctuate the deeply restful and natural interior, including Louis Grant's purple
and pink pastel square works, *A delicate point of view* (opposite) and (top right).

THE FINISHING TOUCH

.

.

.

"

THE FLOWERS ARE EPHEMERAL.

—— *Lisa Cooper* | *Doctor Cooper Studio* ——

Flowers, fruit, vegetables, ribbons and even leavened bread take on a life of their own in florist, artist and doctor of philosophy Lisa Cooper's talented hands. As she finishes each composition, she places it on a plinth to document, 'letting it go live its life', marking its completion and freeing up valuable headspace for her next work.

Flowers have been her long-time friends. Her late father was a butcher who viewed his work as akin to sculpture. It gave rise to Cooper's unique view of flowers as a slide between art and trade.

'There was a lot of intense philosophical discussion about the grace of living and dying,' she says. 'And to me, flowers are the greatest wisdom available to us.'

Her work transcends still life, expressing beauty that feels indescribable, in a similar vein to a material wedding ring being a symbol of love, but the love itself being undefinable.

'The things we really take into our souls are those things that cannot be held or kept, such as people, animals and, for me, the flowers,' she says.

She works by intuition, feeling compelled towards things so strongly that she works first and figures out why later. In the composition illustrated, the botanical elements appear to move despite sitting still on the ledge, bridging the gap between life and death.

'Everyone wanted to commission the same thing after seeing that,' she laughs. 'I think it was because it felt like the wind was whipping through the grass ... The flowers definitely have an energy.'

———

Lisa Cooper's composition on its white platform opposite, adding the final flourish in a time-honoured tradition of floral embellishment.

PROJECT CREDITS

 ANCIENT GROUNDING
STONE SOUL HOUSE

ARCHITECT | Robson Rak Architecture & Interiors
INTERIORS | Robson Rak Architecture & Interiors
STYLIST | Tamara Maynes
LANDSCAPE | Landspace Landscaping and Cos Design
BUILDER | LBA Construction

10   Maringka Baker, *Minyma kutjara tjukurpa*, 2019
      Synthetic polymer paint on linen, 120 x 200 cm
      Courtesy of Vivien Anderson Gallery, Melbourne

      Danielle Thiris, *This Pot May Tickle Your Funny Bone*, 2022
      Terracotta, slips, terra sigilata, oxides and mid fire glaze materials, 18 x 29 cm
      Acquired by Hotel Vera, Ballarat

12   John Young, *Aleph*, 2021
      Oil on Belgian linen, 203 x 370 cm
      Courtesy of artist and Olsen Gallery, Sydney

21   Helen Redmond, *Kunsthalle*, 2022
      Oil on canvas, 77 x 134 cm
      Courtesy of Otomys, Melbourne

      Sally Kent, *Ball vase*, 2022
      Handbuilt stoneware ceramic, 37 x 23 cm

      Sally Kent, *Large spiky vase*, 2022
      Handbuilt stoneware ceramic, 25 x 23 cm

      Clae Studio, *Drum vessel in matte white*, 2021
      Ceramic, glaze, 21 x 15 cm

22   Greg Wood, *V6 Nature of Change*, 2021
      Oil on linen board, 61 x 92 cm
      Courtesy of Otomys, Melbourne

 LIGHT TOUCH
COLLECTORS DEN

ARCHITECT | Hecker Guthrie
INTERIORS | Hecker Guthrie
STYLING | Hecker Guthrie
BUILDER | Strawco Building

27   Greg Wood, *Mowbrays / Dryden*, 2017
      Oil on canvas board, 28 x 28 cm (each)
      Courtesy of artist and Fletcher Arts, Melbourne

28   Artist unknown, bought at auction (top left)

      Artist unknown, bought at auction (bottom right)

30   Aarre Heinonen, *Still Life*, 1958
      Oil on canvas, 47 x 55 cm
      Vintage artwork from Gallery Midlandia, Melbourne

 LIVING TREASURES
VILLA GLEN

ARCHITECT | Lucy Clemenger Architects
INTERIORS | Lucy Clemenger Architects
STYLIST | Natalie James
BUILDER | Nexus Construction

35   Lisa Roet, *Monkey love sign*, 2016
      Bronze, gold plated, 25 x 20 cm
      Courtesy of artist, Pieces of Eight, Melbourne, Gow Langsford Gallery, Auckland and Fletcher Arts, Melbourne

      Guido Maestri, *Melt*, 2008
      Oil on linen, 183 x 152 cm
      Courtesy of Jan Murphy Gallery, Brisbane and Yavuz Gallery, Sydney

      Miki Taira, *The Foolish Husband and the Mustard Pickles*, 2011
      Linen, sumi-ink, cotton, wood, vinyl sheet, wire, 39.8 x 22.8 x 22.8 cm
      Courtesy of Tokyo Gallery+BTAP, Tokyo & Beijing

      KAWS, *Along the way vinyl figure (grey)*, 2019
      Sculpture, 25.4 x 19.1 x 8.9 cm

36   Lee Kyoung-Hwa, *Ho! Keum River*, 2007
      Mixed media, 163 x 130 cm
      Courtesy of Georgie Bruce Art Advisory, Melbourne

      Joshua Yeldham, *Sooty Owl (Ed. of 25)*, 2019
      Hand-carved pigment print, 156 x 122 cm
      Courtesy of artist and Scott Livesey Gallery, Melbourne and Arthouse Gallery, Sydney

      Danny Chin-Fai Lee, *Mountain and Streams*, 2008
      Stainless steel and iron, 138 x 32 x 28 cm
      Courtesy of Alisan Fine Arts, Hong Kong

      Lee Hyun Sang, *Travel to Western*, 2010
      Digital c-print, 10 x 206 cm
      Courtesy of Georgie Bruce Art Advisory, Melbourne

      Zhang Dali, *AK-47*, 2010
      Acrylic on vinyl, 102 x 82 cm

      Laura Ellenberger, *Untitled*, 2015
      Graphite, ink, wax, mulberry paper, 80 x 60 cm
      Courtesy of M Contemporary, Sydney and Everard Read Gallery, London

39   TSANG Kin-Wah, *Fucking Art Made by the Fucking People and for the Fucking People (blue on white)*, 2012
      Silkscreen and acrylic on canvas, 122 x 122 cm

40   Guido Maestri, *Govett's leap*, 2013
      Oil on linen, 60 x 50 cm
      Courtesy of Jan Murphy Gallery, Brisbane and Yavuz Gallery, Sydney

      Yang Yongliang, *Viridescence Page 02*, 2009
      Epson inkjet print on fine art paper, 44 x 44 cm
      Courtesy of artist and Yang Yongliang Studio

 ETHEREAL HEIGHTS
AVIAN APARTMENT

ARCHITECT | Harry Seidler
INTERIORS | Alicia Holgar Interiors
STYLING | Clare Delmar / Studio CD
BUILDER | Dacro Constructions

44   Jessalyn Brooks, *The Avians*, 2020
      Custom wall mural

47   Matthew Allen, *Sigil#2*, 2017
      Polished granite and joint compound on linen, 40 x 30 x 2 cm
      Courtesy of Sullivan+Stumpf, Melbourne & Sydney

      Sanné Mestrom, *Untitled (Self Portrait, Hazelnuts)*, 2017
      Concrete and bronze, 170 x 128 x 15 cm
      Courtesy of Sullivan+Strumpf, Melbourne & Sydney

      Clay Canoe by Wyan McAllister and Kyle Roddenby, *Lava bottle*, 2019
      Ceramic, 33 x 15 cm
      Courtesy of Clay Canoe, Newcastle

48   Ryan Hoffmann, *RH 245 Downtown, LA (2317 280212)*, 2016
      Moulded oil paint, acrylic polymer, wax, CSM Gypsum, aluminium, timber and stainless steel, 145 x 145 x 25 cm
      Courtesy of artist and Liverpool Street Gallery, Sydney

50   Walter Auer, *Unknown*, n.d
      Sculpture, 60 x 30 cm
      Courtesy of Graphis, Sydney

      Rose Jensen-Holm, *Untitled*, 2017
      Stoneware, porcelain, 31 x 18 cm

      Shelly Witters, *Black bust*, 2015
      Cast glass, 25 x 13 cm
      Courtesy of The Vault, Sydney

51   McLean Edwards, *Art Quartet #4*, 2018
      Ink on paper, 105 x 76 cm
      Courtesy of Olsen Gallery, Sydney

53   Daevid Anderson, *Beauty*, 2017
      Oil on board, 34 x 34 cm
      Courtesy of Lethbridge Gallery, Brisbane

Guido Deleu, *The Visitor*, 2009
Ceramic, 24 x 8 x 6 cm (each)
Courtesy of Gardeco, Belgium and Parterre, Sydney

Guido Maestri, *Ghost*, 2016
Painted bronze, concrete 56 x 17 x 17 cm
Courtesy of Jan Murphy Gallery, Brisbane and Yavuz Gallery, Sydney

WHIMSICAL FEELS
PARKLIFE APARTMENT

INTERIORS | Hecker Guthrie
STYLING | Hecker Guthrie
LANDSCAPE | The Plant Charmer
BUILDER | Dome Builders

54   Julia Ciccarone, *Study for Portal*, 2017
     Oil on board, 33 x 26 cm
     Courtesy of artist and Niagara Galleries, Melbourne

57   Alexandra Standen, *Wedgewood Blue*, 2021
     Handbuilt, lumina porcelain, black clay, glaze, 79 x 36 x 36 cm
     Courtesy of THIS IS NO FANTASY, Melbourne and Chalkhorse, Sydney

58   Del Kathryn Barton, *Oh intervene for us*, 2006
     Mixed media on paper
     Courtesy of artist and Roslyn Oxley9 Gallery, Sydney

60   Julia Ciccarone, *Mesmerised*, 2015
     Oil on board, 25 x 25 cm
     Courtesy of artist and Niagara Galleries, Melbourne

67   David Noonan, *Untitled*, 2005
     Fabric painting, 176 x 114 cm
     Courtesy of artist and Anna Schwartz Gallery, Melbourne

GRAND UNVEILING
THE GLASS HOUSE

ARCHITECT | ADDARC
INTERIORS | ADDARC
STYLING | Swee Lim / Swee Design
LANDSCAPE | Jack Merlo
BUILDER | Lang Construction

70   Guan Wei, *Cloud No.3*, 2012
     Bronze sculpture, 167 x 100 x 90 cm
     Courtesy of ARC ONE Gallery, Melbourne and Martin Browne Contemporary, Sydney

     Bruce Armstrong, *Bunjil*, 2016
     Painted bronze on timber plinth, 245 x 60 cm
     Courtesy of & Gallery, Sorrento

74   Richard Stringer, *The Queen is Dead*, 2019
     Alabaster (composite material), 26 x 20.5 x 19 cm
     Courtesy of artist and Fletcher Arts, Melbourne

75   Paul Wood, *Tiger*, 2011
     Re-fired ceramic and glass, 80 x 60 x 45 cm

     Richard Stringer, *Untitled Maquette*, 2000
     Aluminium Bronze, 23 x 29 x 18 cm
     Courtesy of artist and Fletcher Arts, Melbourne

76   Richard Stringer, *Bee replicas*, 2019
     Alabaster (composite material), 13 x 12 cm (each)
     Courtesy of artist and Fletcher Arts, Melbourne

     Marnie Haddad, *'The Apartment' Untitled #2*, 2016
     Digital type-c photography, 120 x 180 cm
     Courtesy of artist and Fletcher Arts, Melbourne

     Kirby Bourke, *Monolith 3*, 2021
     Brass, 75 x 40 x 40 cm
     Courtesy of artist and Fletcher Arts, Melbourne

     Peter D Cole, *2023 – Journey*, 2023
     Brass, 70 x 8 cm
     Courtesy of Fletcher Arts, Melbourne

79   Richard Stringer, *Table Mountain*, 2002
     Aluminium Bronze, 158 x 65 x 50 cm
     Courtesy of artist and Fletcher Arts, Melbourne

HERITAGE SECRETS
COBDEN TERRACE

ARCHITECT | Matt Gibson Architecture + Design
INTERIORS | Matt Gibson Architecture + Design
STYLING | Matt Gibson Architecture + Design
LANDSCAPE | Robyn Barlow Design
BUILDER | Kleev Homes

83   Henrietta Zeffert, *Sasha*, 2002
     Charcoal on paper, 62 x 92 cm

84   Nic Plowman, *Avalanche #3*, 2020
     Mixed media on paper, 42 x 29.7 cm
     Courtesy of James Makin Gallery, Melbourne

88   Artist unknown (top right)

     Danny Cohen, *Hyena*, 2010
     Photograph
     Courtesy of artist and National Portrait Gallery, Canberra

89   Greg Wood, *V2 Reimagining*, 2020
     Oil on linen, 80.5 x 140 cm
     Courtesy of Otomys, Melbourne

91   Stephanie Rampton, *Untitled*, 2013
     Print, 20 x 25 cm
     Courtesy of artist and Australian Galleries, Melbourne

Robyn Rayner, *Midnight*, 2009
Print, 32 x 28 cm
Courtesy of artist and PG Gallery, Melbourne

HOTEL HOMAGE
BALMERINO RESIDENCE

INTERIORS | Studio Griffiths Architecture + Design
STYLING | Swee Design
LANDSCAPE | by client
BUILDER | by client

93   Craig MacLean, *Grace*, n.d
     Photographic Print, 150 x 100 cm

94   Henry Santoso, *Unknown* (wall sculpture), n.d

     Dawn Vachon, *Thick thaw*, 2022
     Ceramic, 30 x 20 x 22 cm
     Courtesy of pépite, Melbourne

     Anya Pesce, *White Freestanding Form*, 2021
     Hand-moulded polymethyl methacrylate, 35 x 22 x 11 cm
     Courtesy of M Contemporary, Sydney

100 Simone Karras, *Ceramic vessel*, 2023
     Ceramic, 30 x 30 cm
     Courtesy of pépite, Melbourne

     Kirsten Perry, *Backbend*, 2022
     Ceramic, glaze, 35 x 17 x 12 cm
     Courtesy of pépite, Melbourne

101 Angela Hayes, *Ceramic sculpture*, 2022
     Ceramic, 22 x 16.5 x 8.5 cm
     Courtesy of pépite, Melbourne

     Iggy & Lou Lou, *Ceramic Grecian Vase*, 2021
     Ceramic, 34 x 11.5 cm Melbourne
     Courtesy of pépite, Melbourne

     Kirsten Perry, *Folded vase with gold drips*, 2022
     Ceramic, glaze, gold lustre, 16 x 10 x 10 cm
     Courtesy of pépite, Melbourne

     Dawn Vachon, *Mist slip*, 2022
     Ceramic, 22 x 18 x 13 cm
     Courtesy of pépite, Melbourne

PROJECT CREDITS

FEMININE BEAUTY
HAVERBRACK

INTERIORS | Beatrix Rowe
STYLING | Beatrix Rowe
LANDSCAPE | Eckersley Garden Architecture
BUILDER | CBD Contracting Group

111   Shelley Hannigan, *Black dress*, 2021
      Wire, sinamay and thread, 124 x 66 cm

112   Left dress:
      Shelley Hannigan, *Selve-age 7*, 2021
      Copper wire and polyester thread, 116 x 60 cm

      Right Dress:
      Shelley Hannigan, *Anne Drysdale*, 2023
      Copper wire and polyester thread 130 x 80 cm

SALIENT GREEN
EVERGREEN HOUSE

ARCHITECT | Robson Rak Architecture & Interiors
INTERIORS | Robson Rak Architecture & Interiors
STYLIST | Swee Lim
LANDSCAPE | Form Landscaping and Eckersley
Garden Architecture
BUILDER | Leone Construction

116   *Top left*
      Max Bowden, *Alice Springs*, 2021
      Oil on canvas, 30.5 x 30.5
      Courtesy of James Makin Gallery, Melbourne

      Top right
      Sam Michelle, *Vases, flowers & shapes*, 2022
      Oil on canvas, 79 x 79 cm, 79 x 61 cm (left to right)
      Courtesy of Gallerysmith, Melbourne

      Bottom
      Belynda Henry, *Golden*, 2018
      Oil on canvas, 107 x 122 cm
      Courtesy of artist and Australian Galleries,
      Melbourne & Sydney

      Noel McKenna, *Casper*, 2019
      Oil on board, 40 x 60 cm
      Courtesy of Niagara Galleries, Melbourne

      Lisa Lapointe, *Totem*, 2017
      Timber, acrylic and mixed media 40 x 10 x 10 cm

120   Mark Rodda, *Debris floating on a golden sea*, 2010
      Oil on wood panel, 70 x 170 cm
      Courtesy of Gallery 9, Sydney

124   Mark Roper, *Arcane*, 2017
      Archival pigment print, 100 x 74.8 cm
      Courtesy of artists and Otomys, Melbourne
      Fleur Stevenson, *Sunset Over Wallaby Rocks*, 2020
      Acrylic and spray paint on board, 42 x 42 cm
      Courtesy of artist and The Corner Store Gallery,
      Orange

SPATIAL RESONANCE
WALDEN SHED

ARCHITECT | Noxon Architects
INTERIORS | Noxon Architects
STYLING | Natalie James
LANDSCAPE | Florian Wild, Formed Landscapes and
Noxon Architects
BUILDER | Noxon Architects

FRAMING LANDSCAPES
WOODSMITH ESTATE

ARCHITECT | Abe McCarthy Architects
INTERIORS | Abe McCarthy Architects in
collaboration with AV-ID
STYLING | Natalie James
LANDSCAPE | Barber
BUILDER | GStruct Group

139   Graeme Altmann, *Returning the sound to the sea*, n.d
      Bronze sculpture, 52 x 48 x 12 cm

OPEN EMBRACE
CUNNINGHAM RESIDENCE

ARCHITECT | studiofour
INTERIORS | studiofour
STYLING | studiofour
LANDSCAPE | studiofour
BUILDER | UWood Constructions

148   Marleen Kleiberg, *The Alps*, 2018
      Oil paint on canvas, 20 x 20 cm (each)

LIGHT RELIEF
THE WHITE HOUSE

ARCHITECT | Bower Architecture & Interiors
INTERIORS | Bower Architecture & Interiors
STYLING | Tara Wood & Ruth Welsby
LANDSCAPE | Monique Ho, Autumn Graphics
BUILDER | Ben Gale, Macasar Building

154   *Top right*
      Holly Wilmeth, *'Corazon' Mexico*, 2010
      Photograph, 73 x 50 cm
      Courtesy of artist and San Miguel de Allende,
      Mexico

      Bottom left
      Marta Bonilla, *Terracotta vase*, 2022
      Terracotta, clay, 23 x 20 cm

      Megan Grant, *Miami Brown*, 2020
      Acrylic on board, 42 x 32 cm

STILL LIFE
FOREST GLADE

ARCHITECT | Robert Mills Architecture & Interiors
INTERIORS | Robert Mills Architecture & Interiors /
Swee Lim
STYLING | Swee Lim

156   Emily Ellis, *Raku Speckle Amphora*, 2023
      Raku clay, white stoneware glaze, 40 x 30 cm
      Courtesy of artist and pépite, Melbourne

      Mali Taylor, *Ceramic orbit vase*, 2022
      Stoneware and glaze, 20 x 16.5 cm
      Courtesy of pépite, Melbourne

      Mali Taylor, *Bloom ceramic vase*, 2022
      Stoneware and glaze, 23 x 15 cm
      Courtesy of pépite, Melbourne

      Scott McNeil, *Sculpture #12*, 2022
      Brown stoneware, 20 x 8 cm
      Courtesy of artist and Fletcher Arts

      Rina Bernabei, *Drip bowl*, 2022
      Ceramic, 10 x 26 cm
      Courtesy of artist and pépite, Melbourne

159   Ella Bendrups, *Stacked figure*, 2022
      Scarva stoneware clay, 41 x 12 cm
      Courtesy of artist and pépite, Melbourne

160   Studiopepe, *Ottilie pink vase*, 2019
      Portugal Pink marble, 17 x 29.5 cm
      Courtesy of artist and Bloc Studios, Italy

      Studiopepe, *Eduard white vase*, 2019
      White Carrara marble, 14 x 38 cm
      Courtesy of artist and Bloc Studios, Italy

      Bottom left
      Objects of Common Interest, *OCI Totem I*, 2018
      Portugal Pink, White Carrara, Green Jade and Noir
      Antique marble, 72 x 53 cm
      Courtesy of artist and Bloc Studios, Italy

161   *Bottom left*
      Moli Carew, *Nesting 2*, 2022
      Mixed media, collage on Fabriano, 72 x 53 cm
      Courtesy of artist and Queenscliff Gallery,
      Queenscliff

      Joseph Turrin, *Dragon moon*, 2022
      Stoneware, glaze, 20 x 20 cm
      Courtesy of Turrin Designs and pépite, Melbourne

      Pretziada Studio & Walter Usai, *Mariga Vase*, 2019
      Hand-thrown terracotta, unleaded glaze, hand-
      painted detail, 40 x 27 x 27 cm

162   Sam Michelle, *Pink Heath & Tasmanian Blue Gum*,
      2022
      Oil on canvas, 152 x 143 cm
      Courtesy of Gallerysmith, Melbourne

PROJECT CREDITS

217 Mitch Fong for DenHolm, *Daisy*, 2020
South Australian limestone

Louis Grant, *I'm trying to keep away from you* and
I like to feel my bones when they crash into my heart,
2023
Hot cast, blown and cold worked glass, 21 x 29 cm
(variable)
Courtesy of Fletcher Arts, Melbourne

DOWN TO EARTH
RIVER HOUSE

INTERIORS | Beatrix Rowe
STYLING | Beatrix Rowe
BUILDER | VCON

219 William Jungala King, *Movement of the Earth (brown)*,
2005
Acrylic on linen, 120 x 180 cm
Courtesy of Murphy Art, Sydney

223 Jimmy Donegan, *Unknown*, n.d
Polymer paint on canvas
Courtesy of Ninuku Arts, Kalka

SPIRITED SPEAKING
SACKVILLE LOFT

INTERIORS | Sharon Patsiotis
STYLING | Sharon Patsiotis

228 Harley Manifold, *Commission for Sharon Patsiotis*,
2017
Oil on Belgian linen, 60 x 90 cm

229 *Top left*
Kyoko Imazu and Damon Kowarsky, *Rat*, 2014
Etching and aquatint, 30 x 26 cm
Courtesy of artists and Australian Galleries,
Melbourne

ENGLISH SENSIBILITIES
PIMLICO TERRACE

ARCHITECT | Brayshaw Architects
INTERIORS | Hecker Guthrie
STYLING | Hecker Guthrie
BUILDER | Dome Building

231 Lindsay Blamey, *Lemongum*, 2023
Archival pigment print, 165 x 145 cm
Courtesy of artist and Otomys, Melbourne

235 Ben Mazey, *Black Line Flag Crayon Diptych*, 2022
Ceramic, 65 x 205 cm
Courtesy of C. Gallery (Criteria Collection),
Melbourne

Other featured artwork is the client's own

236 Laura Vahlberg, *Five trees*, 2021
Oil on canvas board, 12.7 x 31 cm
Courtesy of artist and Otomys, Melbourne

Laura Vahlberg, *Van and Snow*, 2022
Oil on canvas board, 22.8 x 31 cm
Courtesy of artist and Otomys, Melbourne

URBAN OASIS
HIDDEN HOUSE

ARCHITECT | Eliza Blair Architecture
INTERIORS | Studio MKN
STYLING | Bea Lambos/ Bea & Co
LANDSCAPE | Mud Office
BUILDER | Kleev Homes

242 Susan Romyn, *Drawing Breath IV*, 1997
Etching, 45 x 40 cm
Courtesy of Eagles Nest Fine Art Gallery, Aireys
Inlet

Carlo Golin, *Ground Works*, 2023
Recycled packaging and paint on board,
23 x 30 cm
Courtesy of Fletcher Arts, Melbourne

245 *Bottom*
Irene Grishin-Selzer, *Clay tablet*, 2023
Ceramic artwork, 33 x 33 cm
Courtesy of artist and pépite, Melbourne

246 Caroline Walls, *Curve IV*, 2021
Silkscreen on fine art paper, 76 x 56 cm

Louis Grant, *A delicate point of view (f)* and *(h)* (left
to right), 2023
Kiln formed and cold worked glass, painted box
frames, 22 x 22 x 35 cm (each)
Courtesy of Fletcher Arts, Melbourne

Martin King, *Both ways*, 2015
Etching and watercolour on paper and drafting
film, 45 x 45 cm
Courtesy of Australian Galleries, Melbourne and
King Street Gallery on William, Sydney

247 *Top right*
Louis Grant, *A delicate point of view (b)*, 2023
Kiln formed and cold worked glass, painted box
frames, 22 x 22 x 35 cm
Courtesy of Fletcher Arts, Melbourne

ACKNOWLEDGEMENTS

It's unusual for a book to have three authors. The three of us have joined to bring our words, images and design together in a creative assemblage, to produce a new language of rooms. We would like to thank everyone who has been part of this book. We are grateful for your energy, interest and encouragement from the first concept to the final page.

ANNIE REID | WORDS

Senior design journalist, writer and author, Annie Reid, has written for over twenty years on design, architecture, property and sustainability with bylines in many leading newspapers and magazines around the world.

She's fascinated by uncovering what's hidden and sharing it respectfully with the world, and through her partnerships with Australia's leading book publishers, agencies and clients, loves the craft of writing and collaboration to bring stories to life.

'To me, a house is not just a series of openings and closings but a curated collection of objects and belongings, from the architects who have built the spaces to the artisans who have crafted the objects and the owners who display them proudly. Grand or small, each gesture speaks across generations, adding layers of detail that bring a house to life.

A spark lights up in me when I have the privilege of observing this in person, and writing about it feeds my deep desire to explore beauty. As a design journalist, I explore life beyond the front door, not only of the people who live there but also of the bricks and mortar themselves. And of course, there are endless stories to tell and bring to the page.

Thank you to our team: Shannon for your incredible talent and for trusting me with your valued clients, Marcus for your digital and design wizardry. To Kirsten Abbott at Thames & Hudson, for your patience and belief in us.

Thank you Eugenie Buchan and Jayne Reid for your book administration and proofing prowess.

Thank you to Ross and our daughters, Lily and Isabelle. I hope you can also create your own joy and magic in the world.'

SHANNON MCGRATH | IMAGES

Shannon McGrath is an award-winning interiors and architecture photographer with twenty-five years' experience, commissioned by pre-eminent architects and designers around Australia. Shannon's work appears often in publications as a regular contributor, and she travels extensively both nationally and overseas photographing buildings and interiors.

She's known for her beautiful portrayal of light and form that celebrates the subject matter, where she continues to glimpse into spaces beyond and the intricacies of what lies beneath.

'This book is about layers of creativity; it is a celebration of wonderful designers and the close relationships that I have formed over many years of photographing their beautiful, interesting, quirky creations.

I have always been interested in discovering the extra elements of a project that emerge when I spend the day with it, especially the makers and creatives. This book has enabled me to celebrate them too.

I have thoroughly enjoyed the collaboration with Annie in skilful words and Marcus's creative genius in his design. Thank you Kirsten Abbott, our wonderful publisher at Thames & Hudson, for letting us run with this book. A thank you to Saskia Pandji Sakti who has worked alongside me in handling my images, your tonal eye is beautiful.

Then, of course, a thank you to my beautiful daughters, Jos and Sybil, for understanding that as a mum and a woman you just need to go for it and create. I'm hoping this will be a good base for them to grow on.

I am incredibly grateful and thankful for this opportunity.'

MARCUS PIPER | DESIGN

Digital Craftsperson, Marcus Piper, has worked across architecture and design titles globally for over two decades picking up awards and recognition for his work at many points along the way.

As the creative force behind many of Australia's leading design titles, he's also art directed publications for the British Crafts Council, Spanish designer Jaime Hayon, Swarovski and the Powerhouse Museum. While he was at it, he has worked alongside some of the world's leading creatives – Neville Brody and Vince Frost – and retains his core values as an industrial designer in creating the publication you hold today as a product of collaboration and physicality.

'It is not lost on me that as a kid I wanted to be an architect. I grew up in the country and was fascinated with technical drawing which resulted in a degree in Industrial Design.

That's how I landed on calling myself a Digital Craftsperson because the pages you are holding are crafted in touch, type and image.

Since then and for twenty-plus years I have been wandering through other people's houses, detailing the work of makers and designers then heralding the work of artists – local and international. All through the lens of you, the reader, bringing a verbal and visual narrative to the pages of numerous magazines and books on architecture and design.

What I have learnt in this time is that great content and collaboration make for amazing publications, and so I applaud my co-creators, Shannon and Annie, then, in-turn, our publisher for their commitment.

Speaking for all of us, we hope you feel inspired as you turn the pages, explore the spaces and put faces to the works.'

assemblage

First published in Australia in 2024
by Thames & Hudson Australia
Wurundjeri Country, 132A Gwynne Street
Cremorne, Victoria 3121

First published in the United Kingdom in 2024
by Thames & Hudson Ltd
181a High Holborn
London WC1V 7QX

First published in the United States of America in 2024
by Thames & Hudson Inc.
500 Fifth Avenue
New York, New York 10110

ISBN 978-1-760-76383-1 (hardback)
ISBN 978-1-760-76462-3 (U.S. edition)

 A catalogue record for this book is available from the National Library of Australia

British Library Cataloguing-in-Publication Data
A catalogue record for this book is available from the British Library

Library of Congress Control Number 2024935640

Every effort has been made to trace accurate ownership of copyrighted text and visual materials used in this book. Errors or omissions will be corrected in subsequent editions, provided notification is sent to the publisher.

Cover photo: Shannon McGrath
Artwork featured on front cover:
Del Kathryn Barton
Oh intervene for us, 2006
Mixed media on paper
Courtesy of the artist and Roslyn Oxley9 Gallery, Sydney

Design: Marcus Piper
Editing: Penny Mansley
Printed and bound in China by C&C Offset Printing Co., Ltd

Thames & Hudson Australia wishes to acknowledge that Aboriginal and Torres Strait Islander peoples are the first storytellers of this nation and the Traditional Custodians of the land on which we live and work. We acknowledge their continuing culture and pay respect to Elders past and present.

Be the first to know about our new releases, exclusive content and author events by visiting

thamesandhudson.com.au   **thamesandhudson.com**   **thamesandhudsonusa.com**